Introduction

Hello my name is Reginald Taylor, the author of this instructional manual. I hope that this manual with my proven art technique inspire many new artists in many new and unexplored paths. This first time published technique has given me a better outlook at producing quality like portraits of others no matter how hard or small your picture may be. If others already label you as an artist. Then why not try to enhance your god given ability by correctly following and using this instructional manual and you will see for yourself the great improvement this art technique will bring to future pictures. Thank you kindly for choosing my book. Enjoy.

List of items needed to construct a few key items in producing quality like portraits:

Cardboard sheet
Ruler
Box knife or razor blade
Ink pen, pencils
Scotch tape
Notebook and printer paper
Scissors
Eraser
2 plastic clear see through sandwich bag not a zip lock, but a regular fold close sandwich bag.

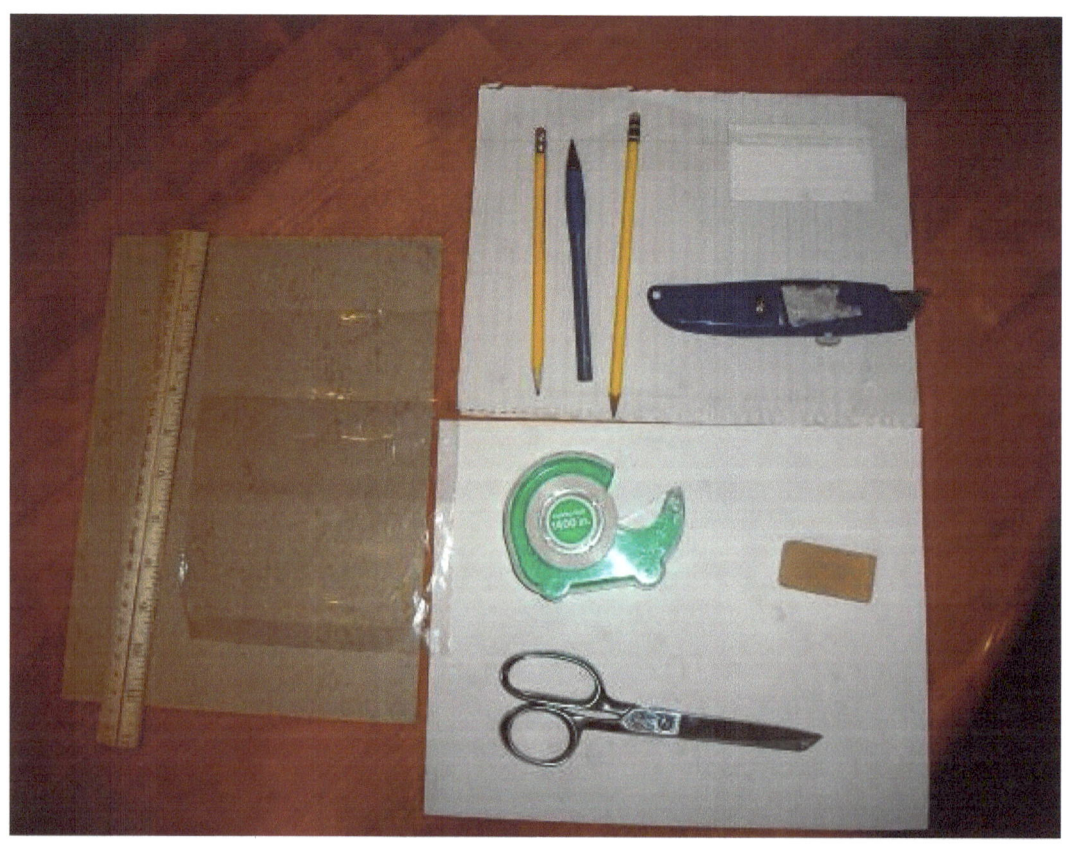

Table of Contents

Chapter 1- making an enlargement ruler – pages 5 – 18

Chapter 2 – how to construct picture holder 1 – pages 19 – 32.

Chapter 3 – how to construct picture holder 2 – pages 33 – 41.

Chapter 4 – how to use items previously constructed items – pages 42 – 48.

Chapter 5 – how to setup your paper – pages 49 – 63.

Chapter 6 – tips on how to construct your own personal shaders– pages 64 – 70.

  Stages of how my portrait was produced pages 71-74.

*Extra are the many different faces that I have done using this exact method and same items we have just constructed.

Chapter 1 – Enlargement ruler

This enlargement ruler will enlarge every portrait you will be drawing in the future. Here are the list of items you will need.

Cardboard sheet
Ink pen
Paper
Ruler

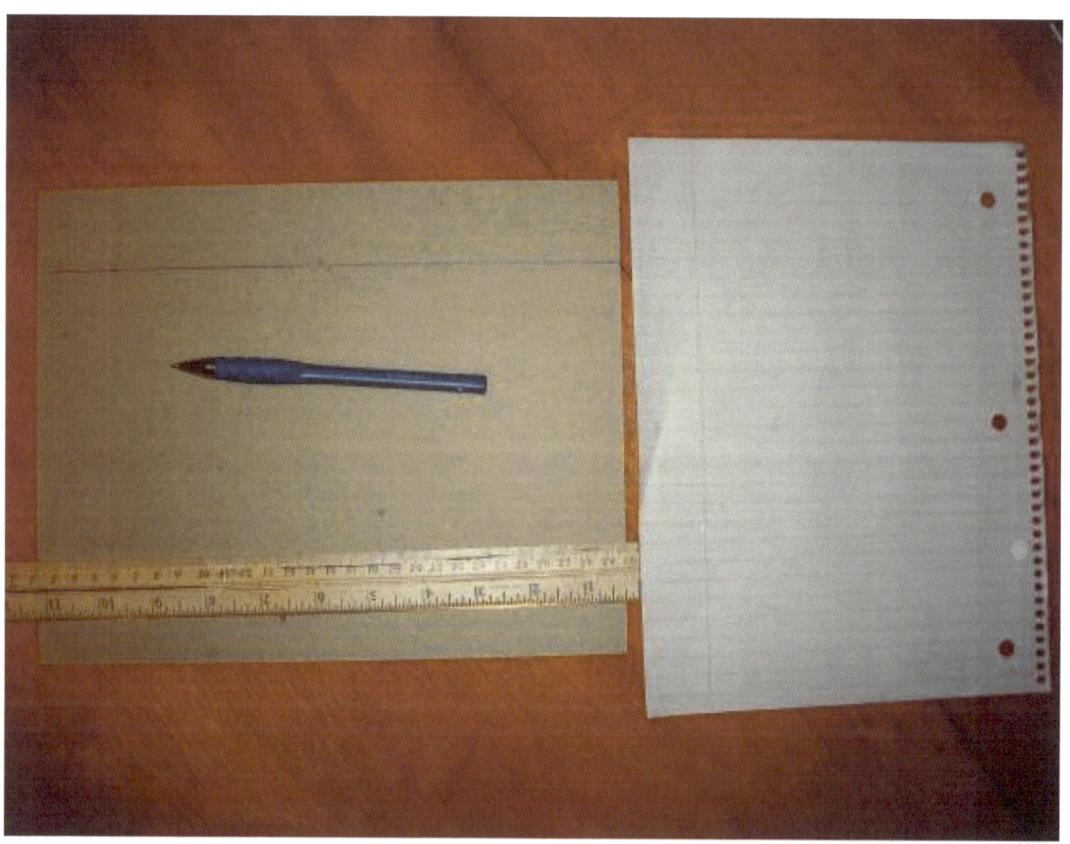

Our first project will be the construction of your cardboard enlargement ruler.

Measure a ruler size of 1 and ½ inch.

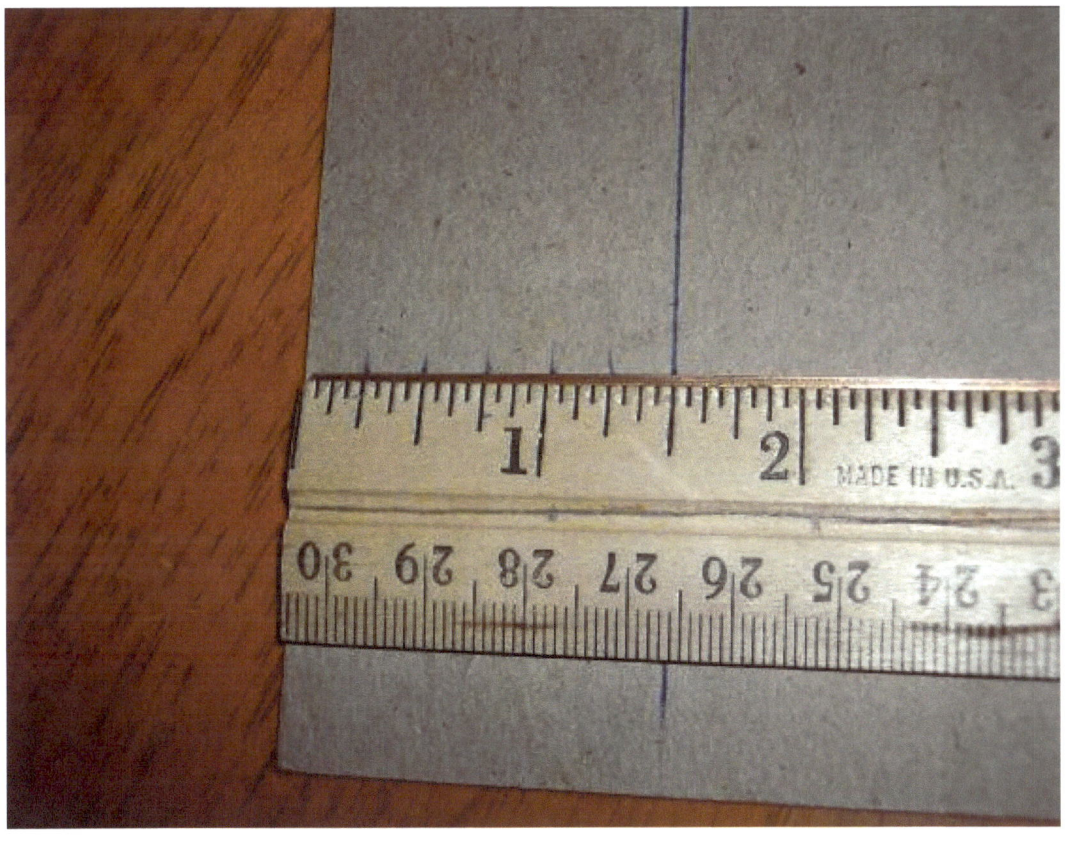

Mark every ¼ inch mark on your ruler on both ends of cardboard paper.

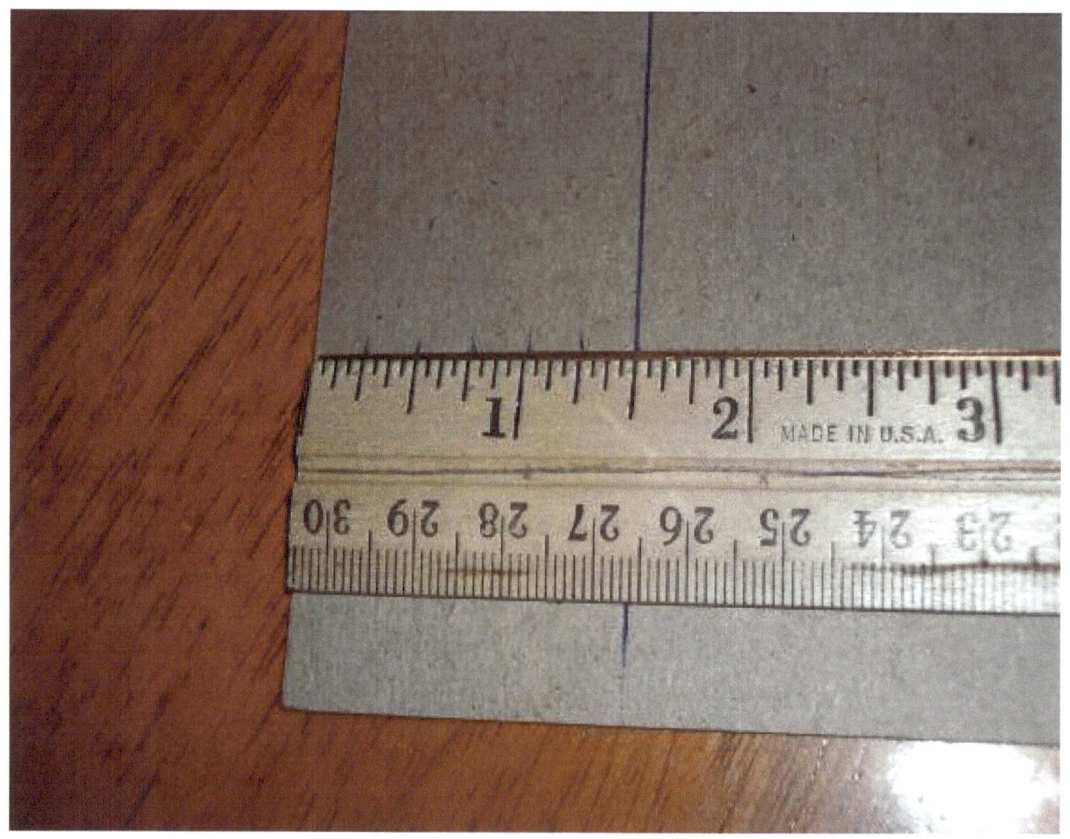

Connect your ¼ inch marks to one another using your ruler.

Align your cardboard ruler with the piece of notebook paper taking care that you have aligned it just as shown below, we will be using the lines located on the paper to construct the first and bottom most row of your cardboard ruler this will be row .

Make sure that your marks are as close and exact to matching the lines on the notebook paper as shown below also remember to do the exact same step to the top of your cardboard ruler.

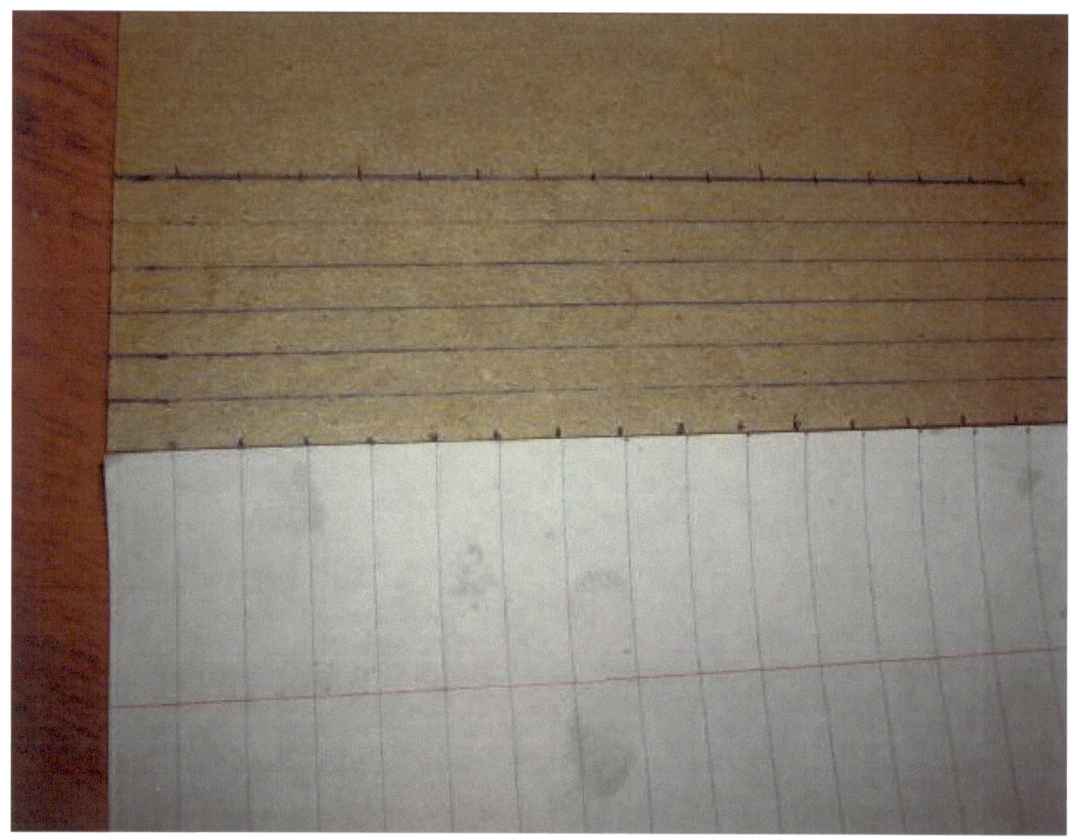

Work from left to right on your ruler, leaving the smaller squares for each row on the far right side of your ruler.

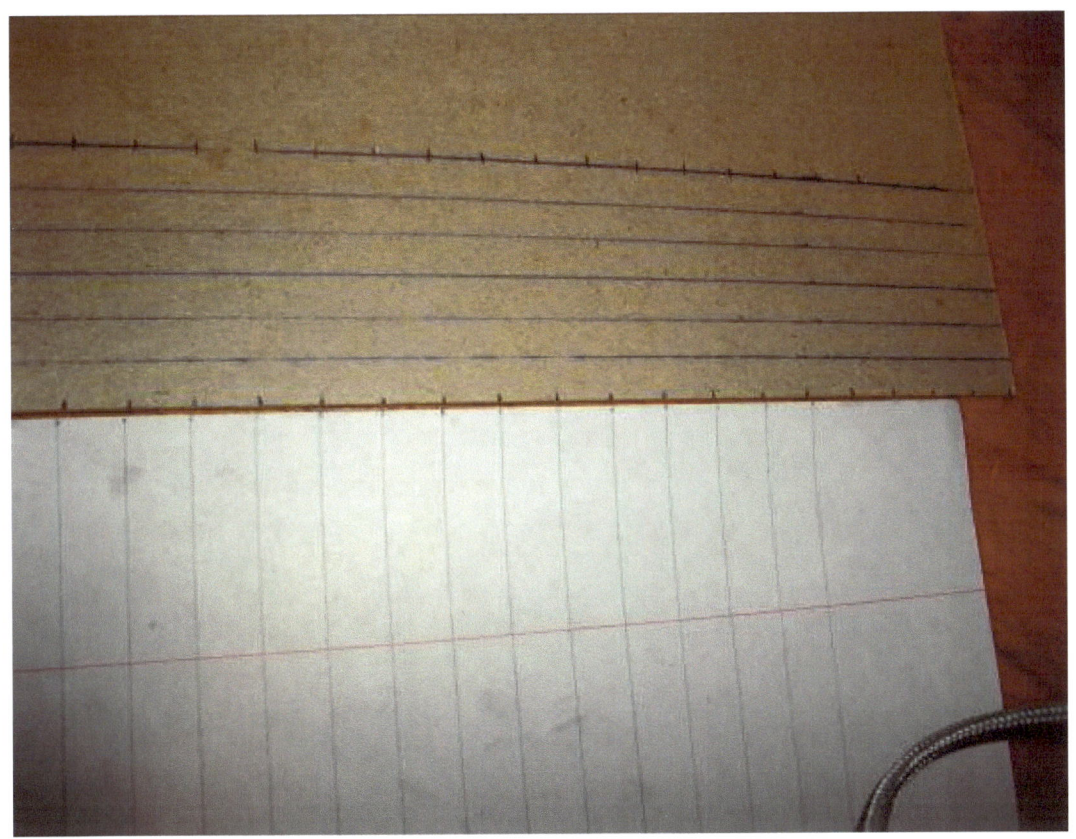

Draw a line using our ruler, connecting the first two lines we made on the bottom and top of our ruler.

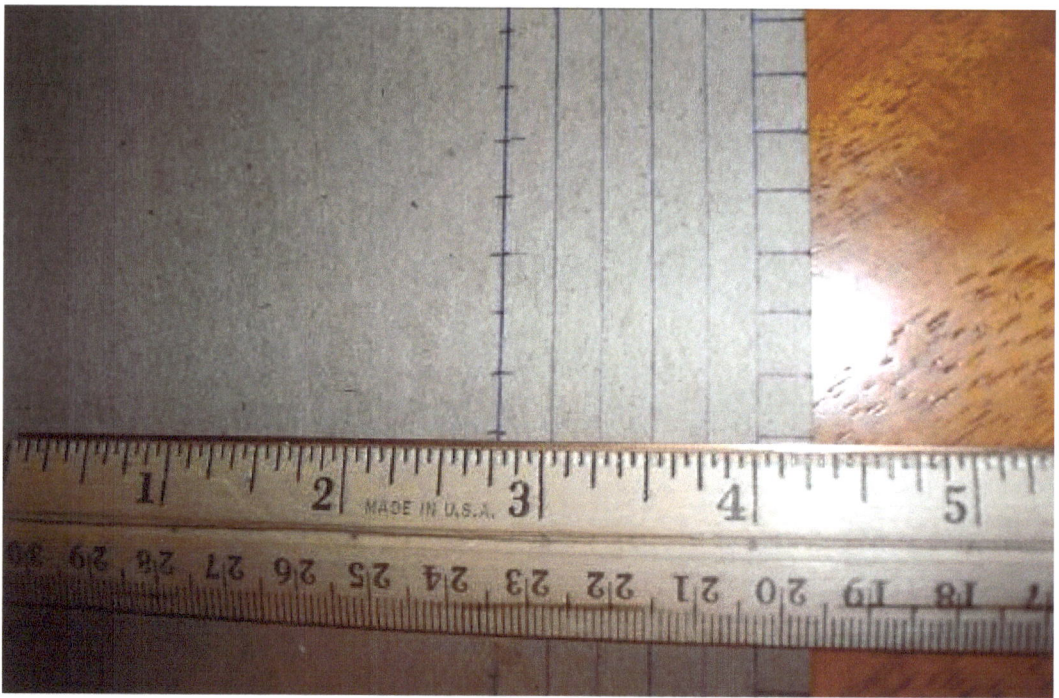

Upon completion of all the lines on your first row (row 1), making a consistent size row 1 blocks completely across your bottom most row of your ruler.

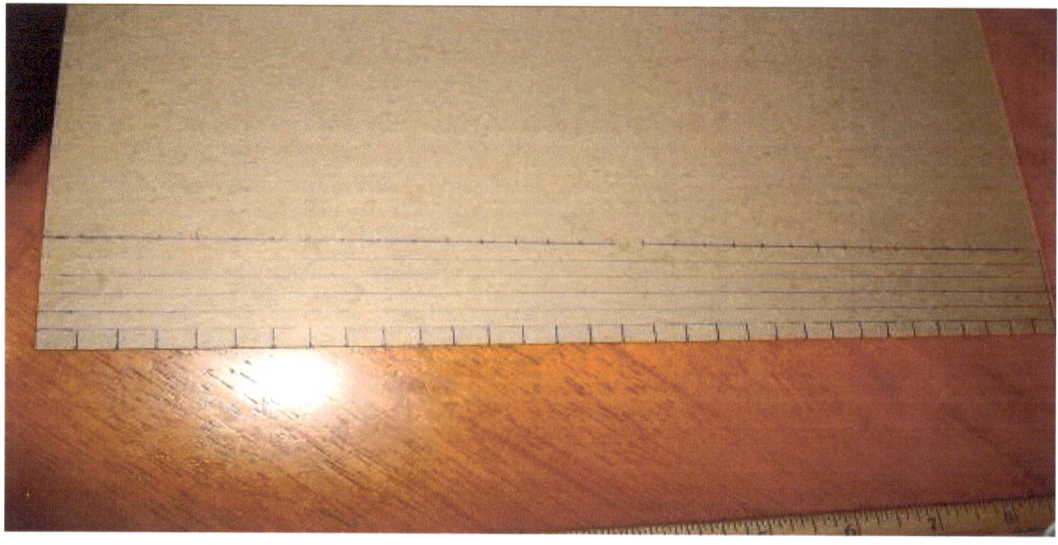

We want to offset the notebook paper as shown below to get the centermost distance point of each square of the first row on your ruler, these center markings will help construct the remaining 5 rows that we will next construct.

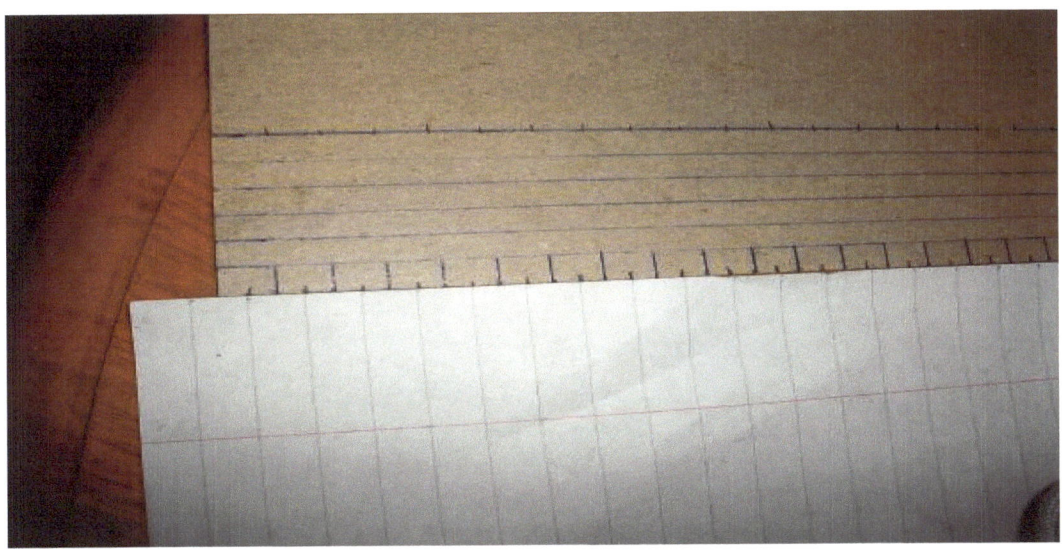

When done with all your center marks, begin to number each block we have just created

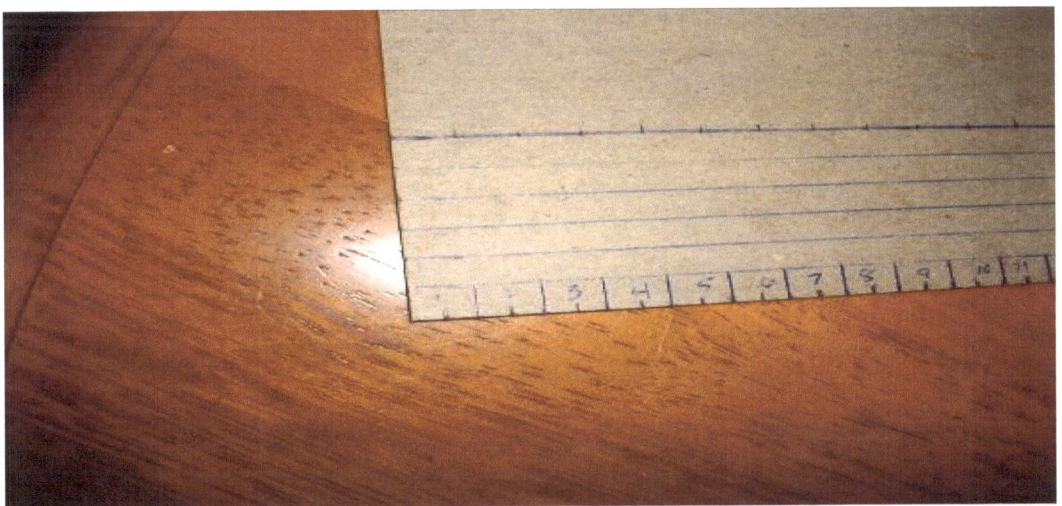

Row 1 will constant of 32 equal blocks.

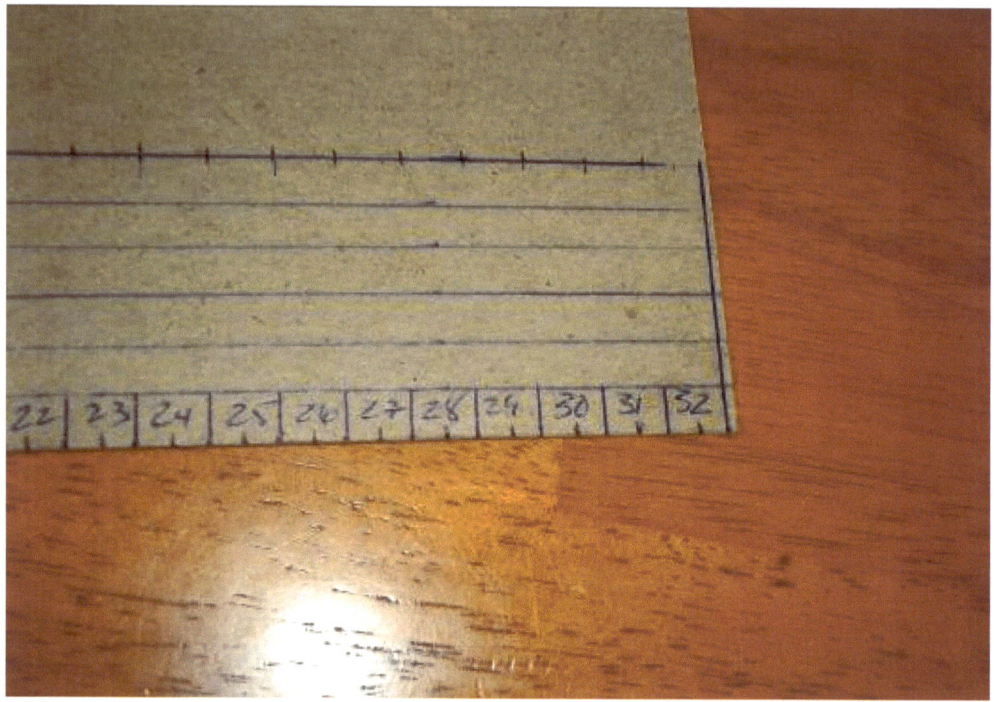

We will construct row 2 of your cardboard ruler counting 3 marks or lines for each block in row 2, remember to count 3 marks for each block on row 2 till the row is filled.

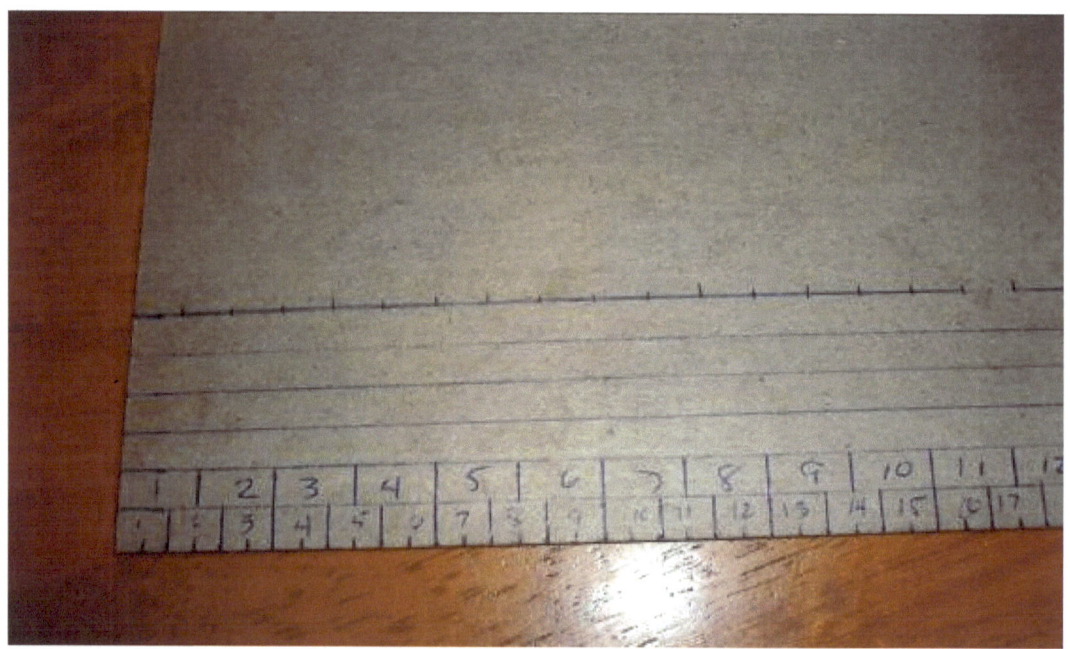

Your ruler should now have two rows with blocks on the second row equal and consistent to the first block of the second row ending with 21 blocks.

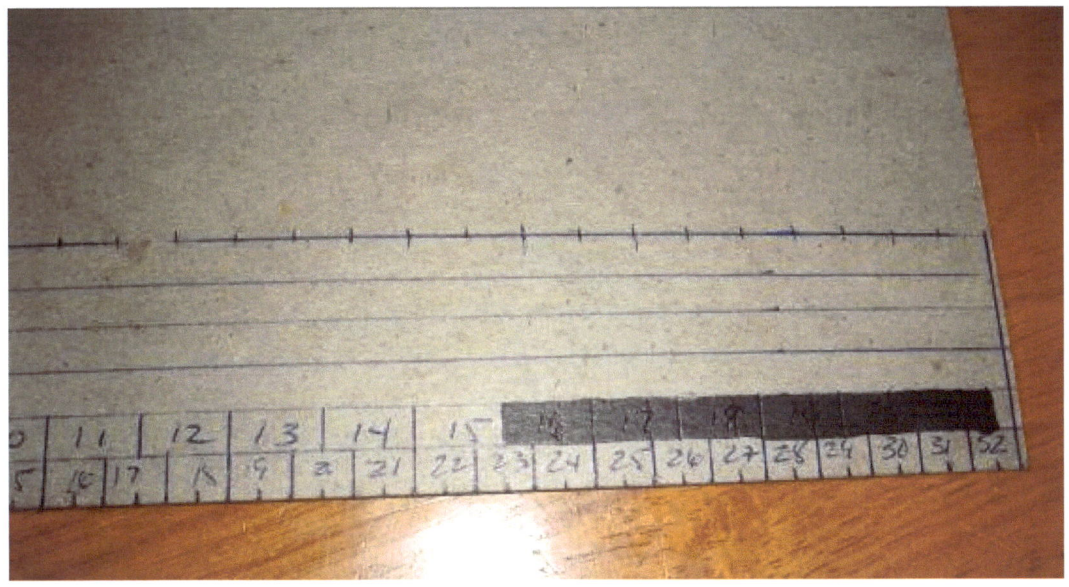

We will begin to construct row 3, row 3 will be 4 times the size of row 1 counting 4 marks per block in row 3.

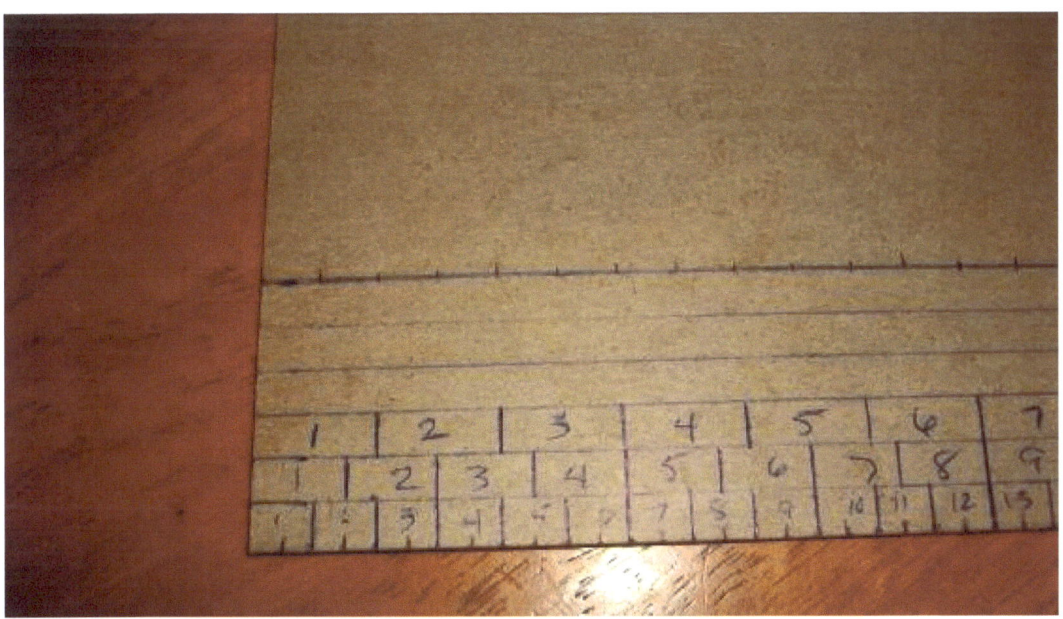

Row 3 should have 16 consistently equal blocks.

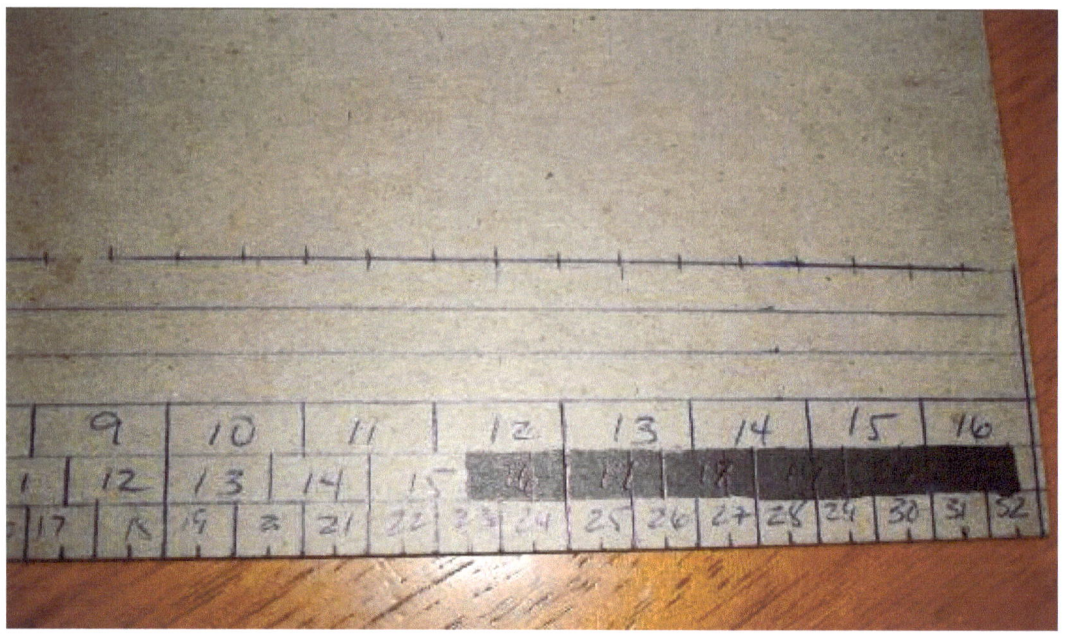

We will repeat the same steps we did for the last two rows only making this row, (row 4) 5 times the size of the first row constructed.

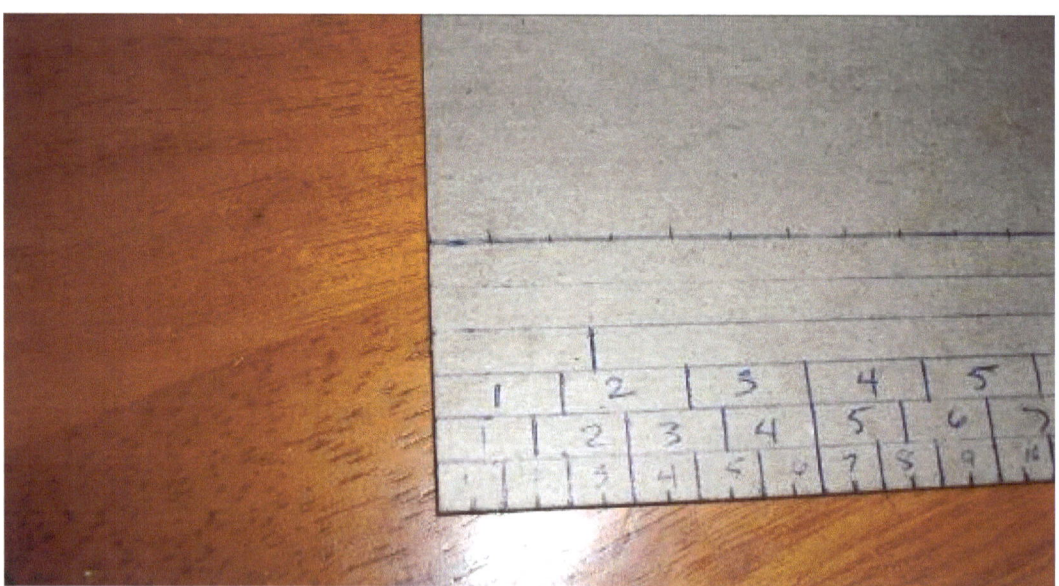

Upon completion row 4 should have 12 consistently equal size blocks.

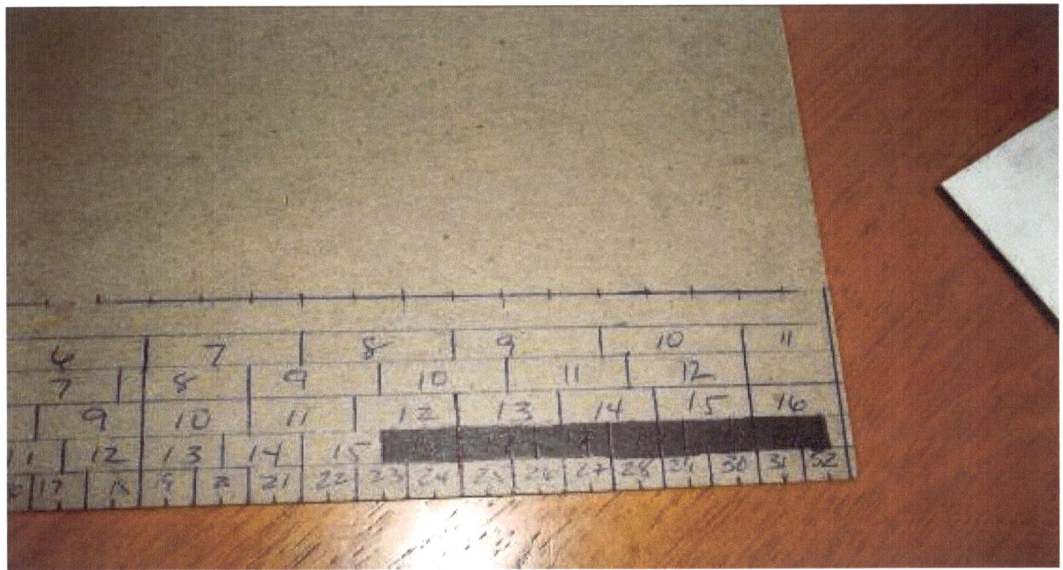

We are ready to construct the last and final row of our cardboard ruler, (row 5) which is 6 times the size the first row constructed, constructing a total of ten equal size blocks for the last and final row to construct.

.

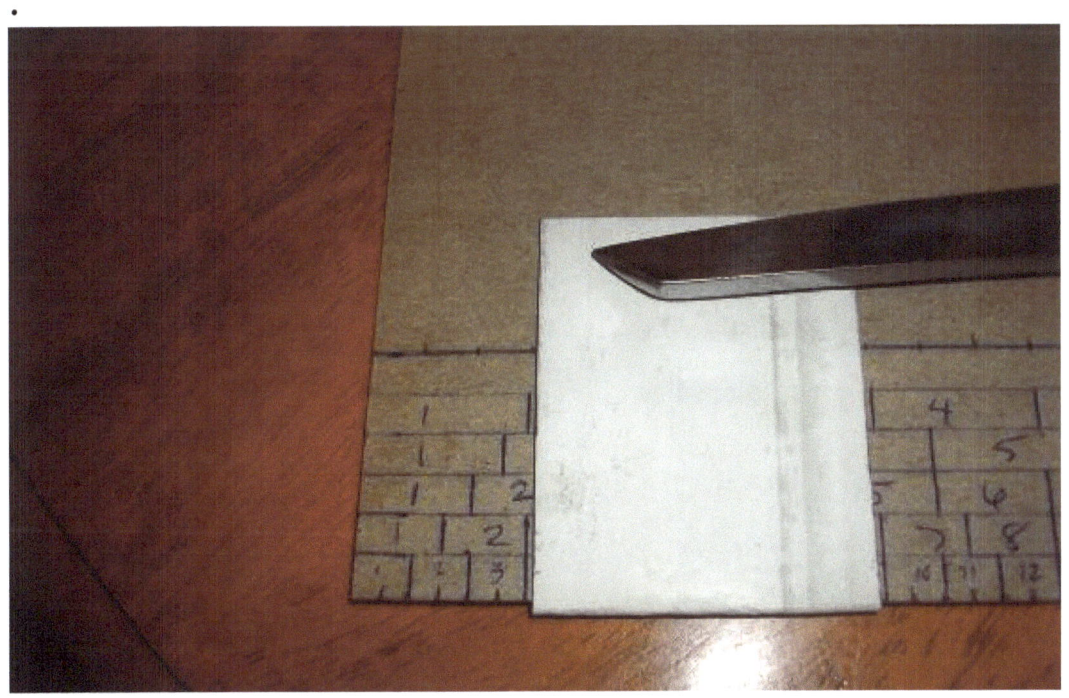

You will have only ten equal consistent blocks not 11.

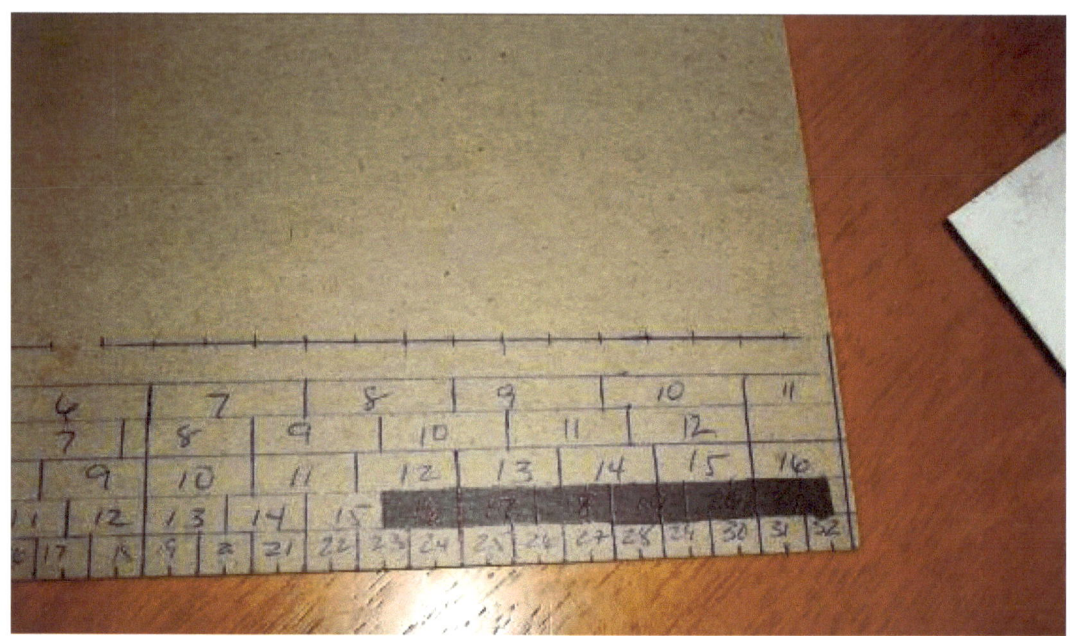

This is our newly constructed picture enlargement ruler which will be used to enlarge the smallest picture to eye catching, sharp and noticeable details of any picture being drawn.

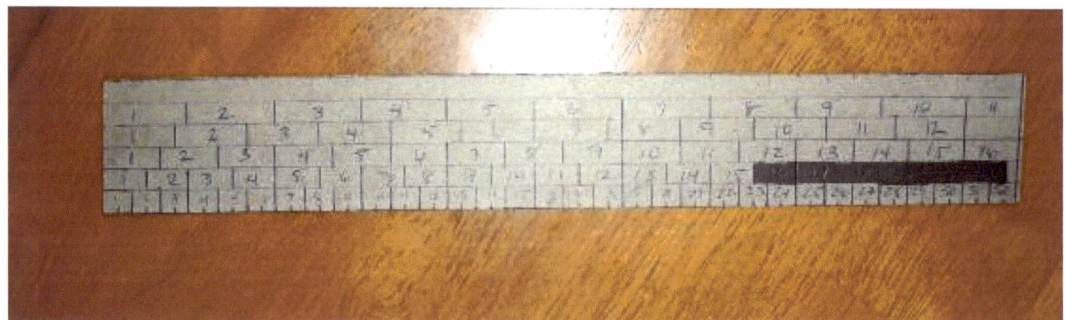

Remember to leave all short and uneven squares on the right side of your new enlargement ruler.

Chapter 2 – picture holder 1

Our next project will be to construct a picture holder. That will be used to cross reference your chosen picture to be drawn. You will need you cardboard that we made our picture holder from, plastic sandwich bag, ink pen, scissors, notebook paper, and tape.

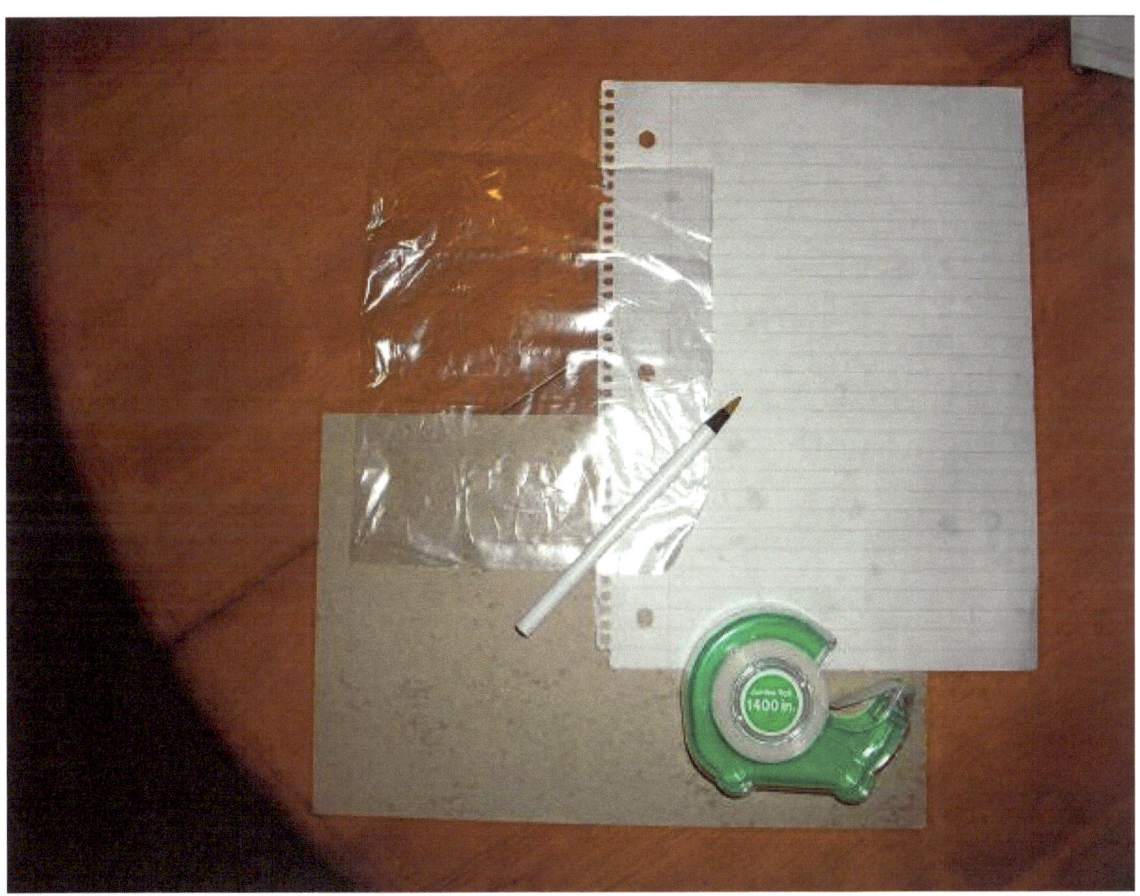

Cut a 5 by 7 piece of cardboard.

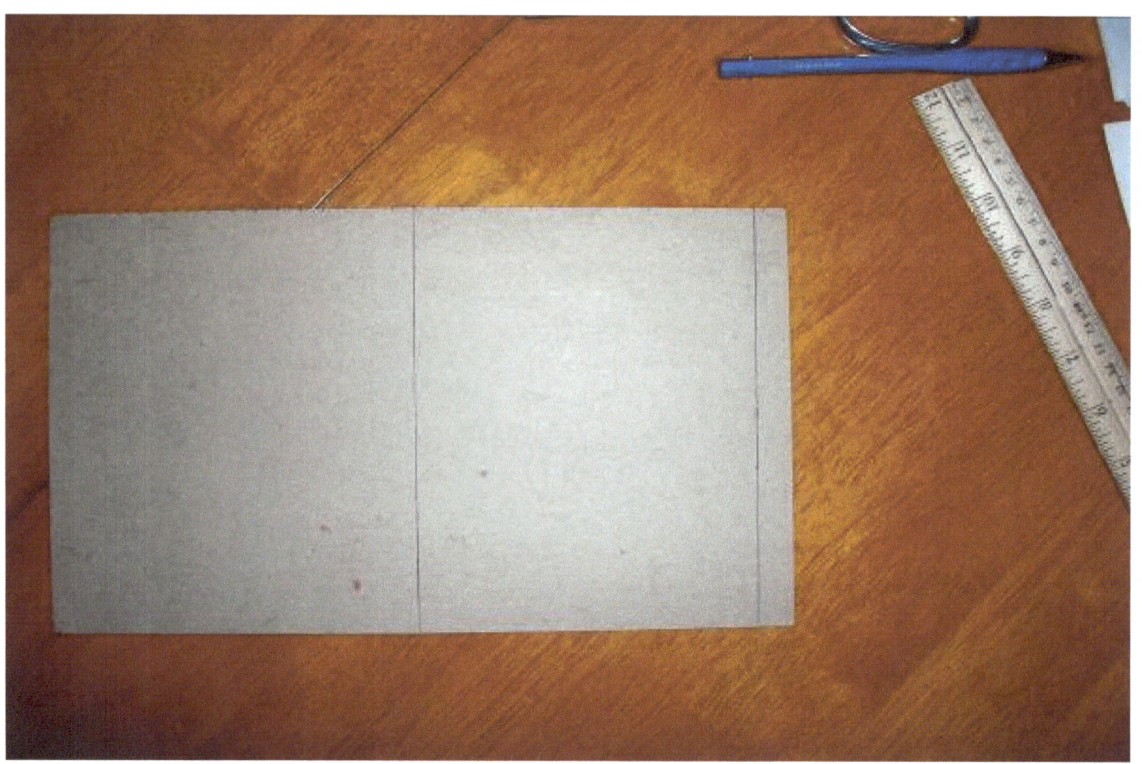

Place your cardboard over your notebook paper, making sure you align the outer edge of your cardboard with the lines on your note book paper.

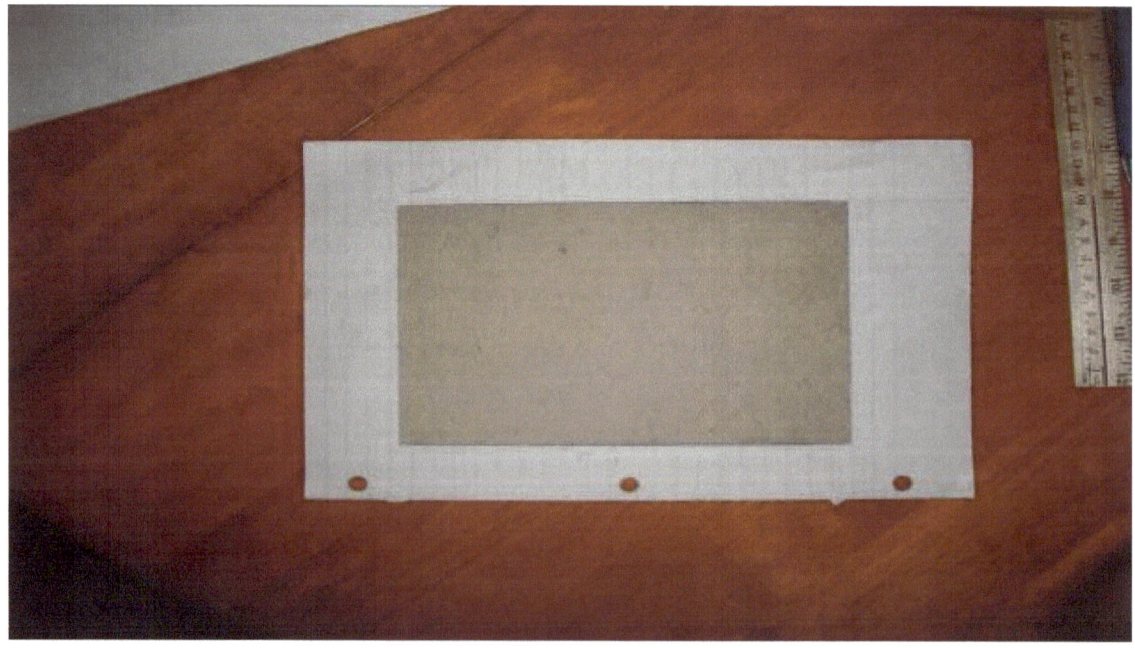

Fold the right and left side of your notebook paper over the cardboard and then tape.

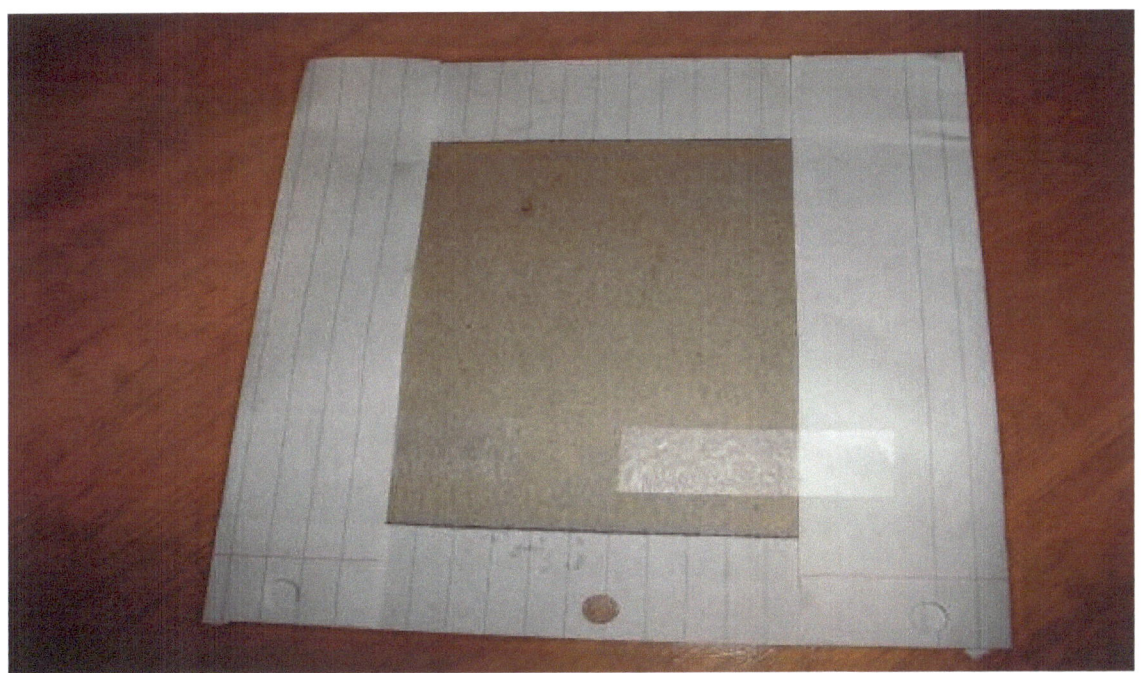

Next fold the top and bottom of your notebook paper over the cardboard then tape.

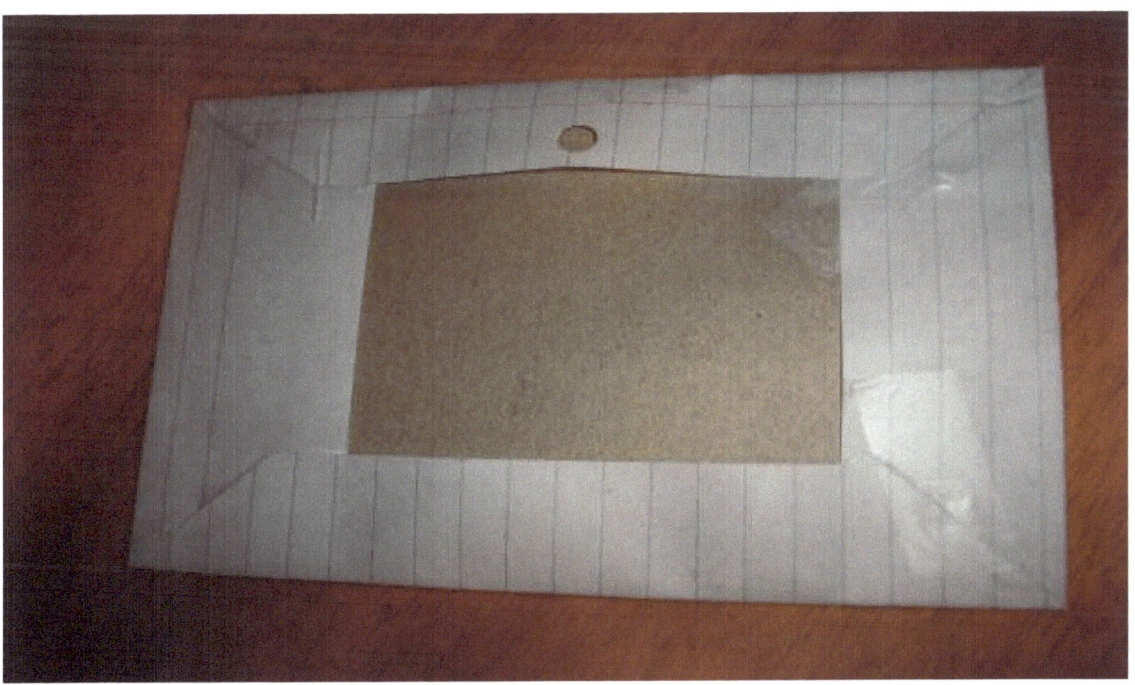

Turn over your newly wrapped cardboard holder.

Place your plastic sandwich bags over your cardboard.

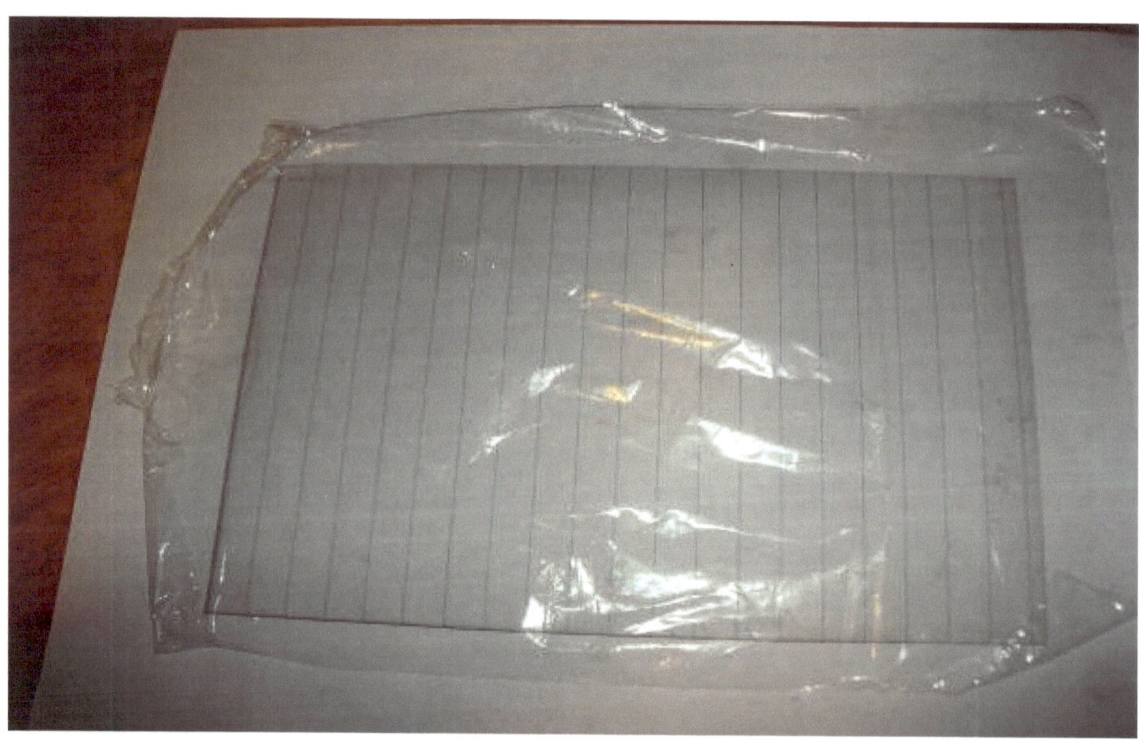

Turn over the cardboard with the plastic on the bottom and your cardboard line side facing down toward the plastic.

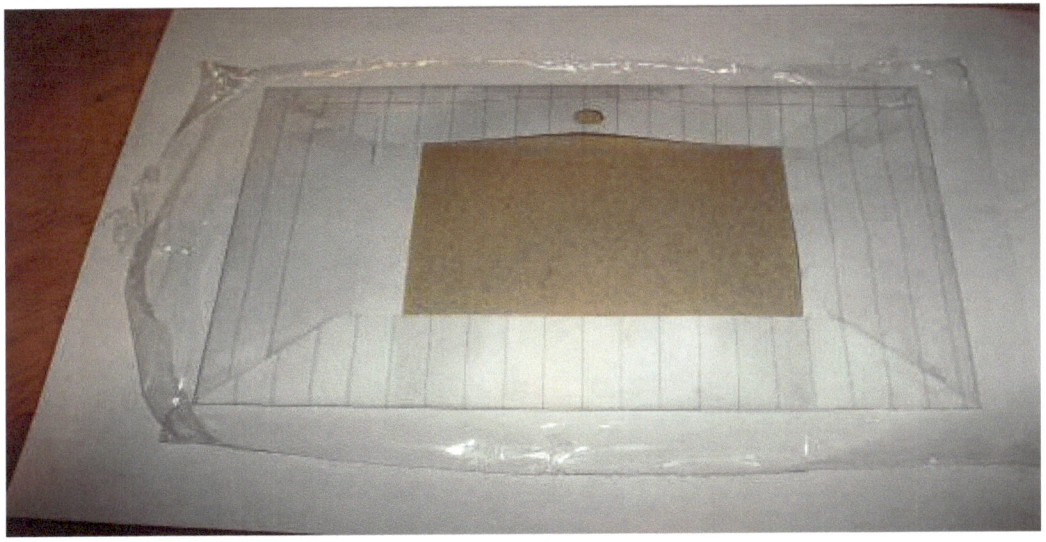

Carefully tape the left and right side of the plastic bag around the cardboard, making sure not to tape your plastic very securely but secure enough so that it won't move, you will soon remove the few pieces of tape that you now use to secure the plastic around the cardboard.

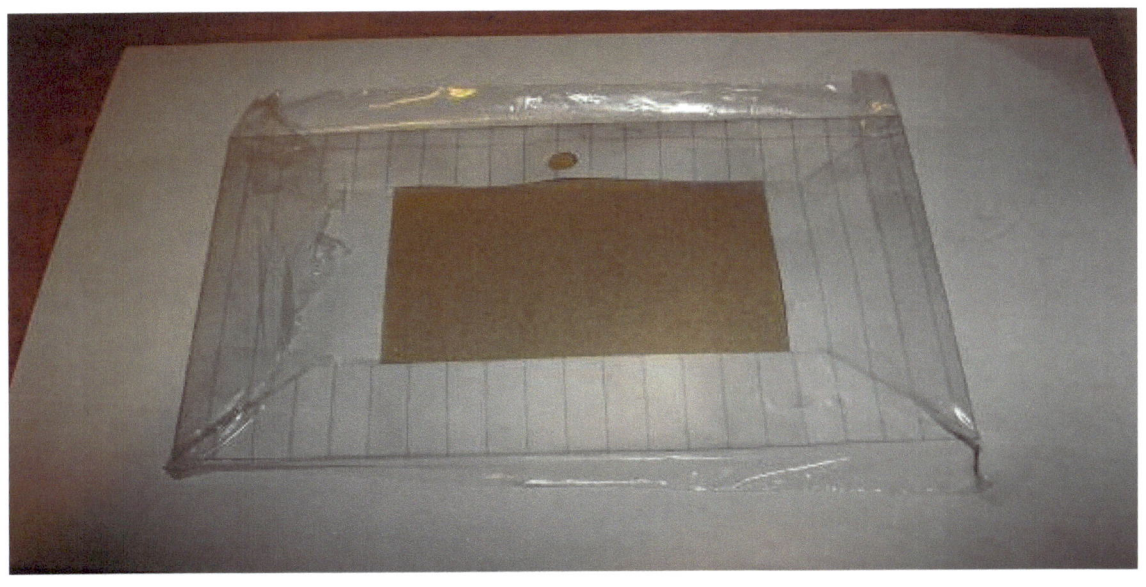

Next we tape the top and bottom of your cardboard.

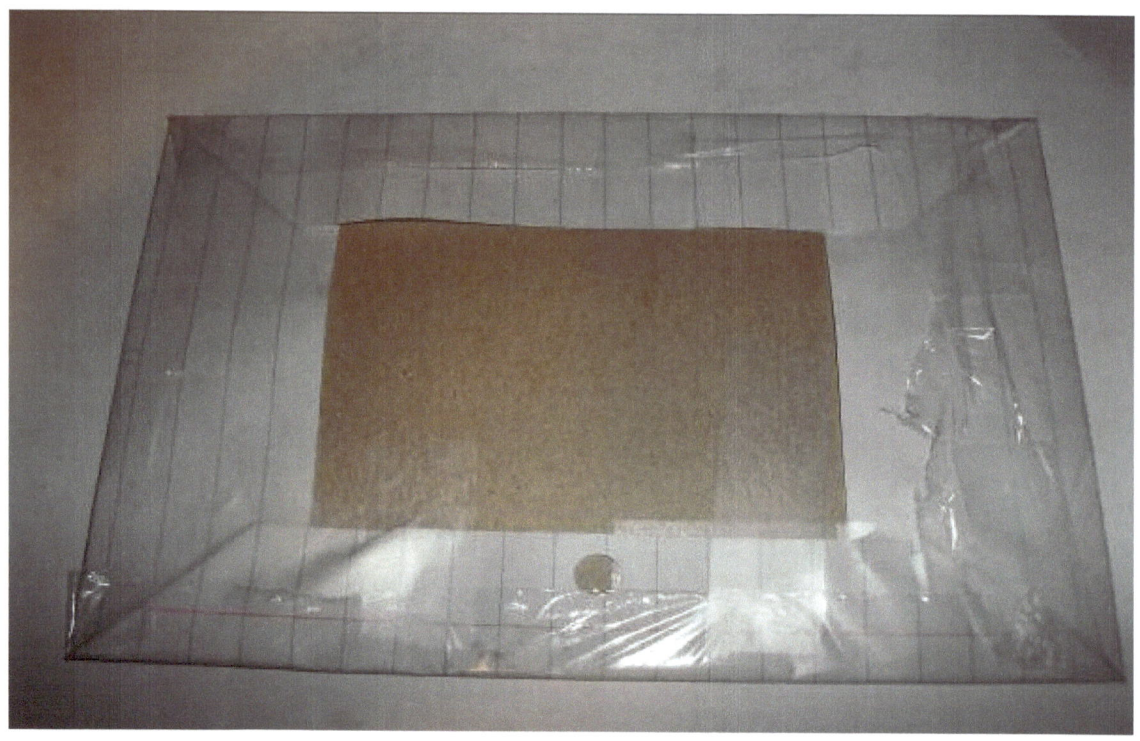

Turn over the cardboard holder.

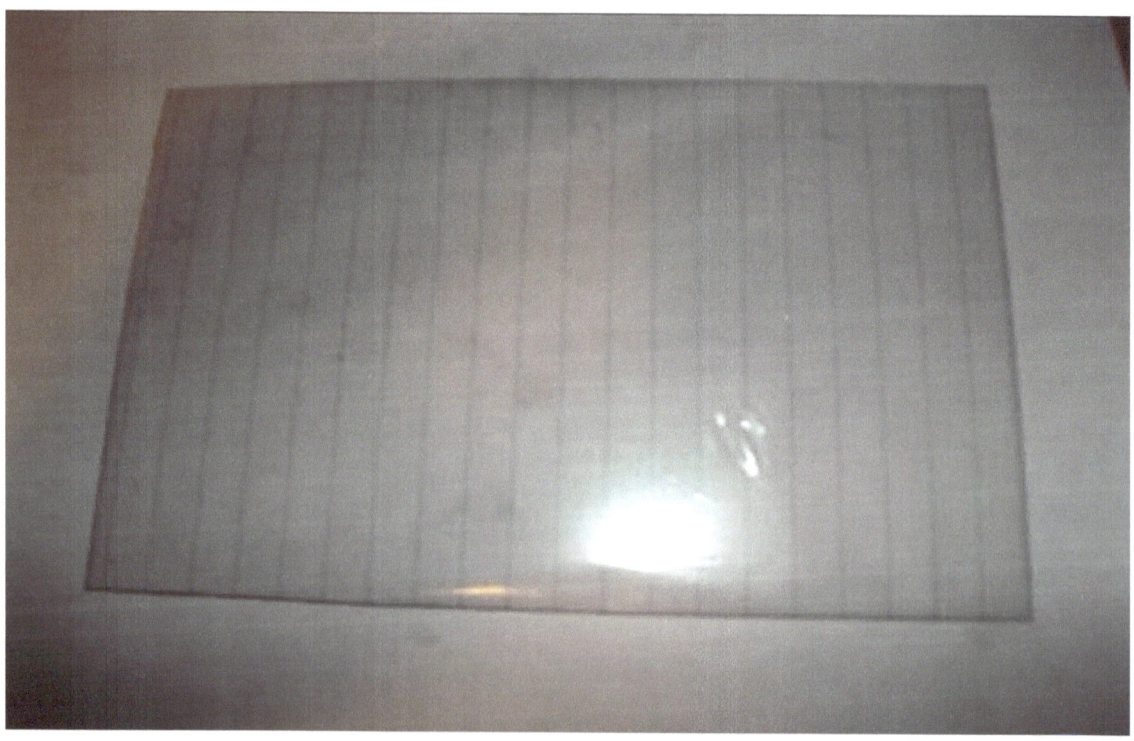

Draw lines using your ruler and ink pen to match the lines on your cardboard holder.

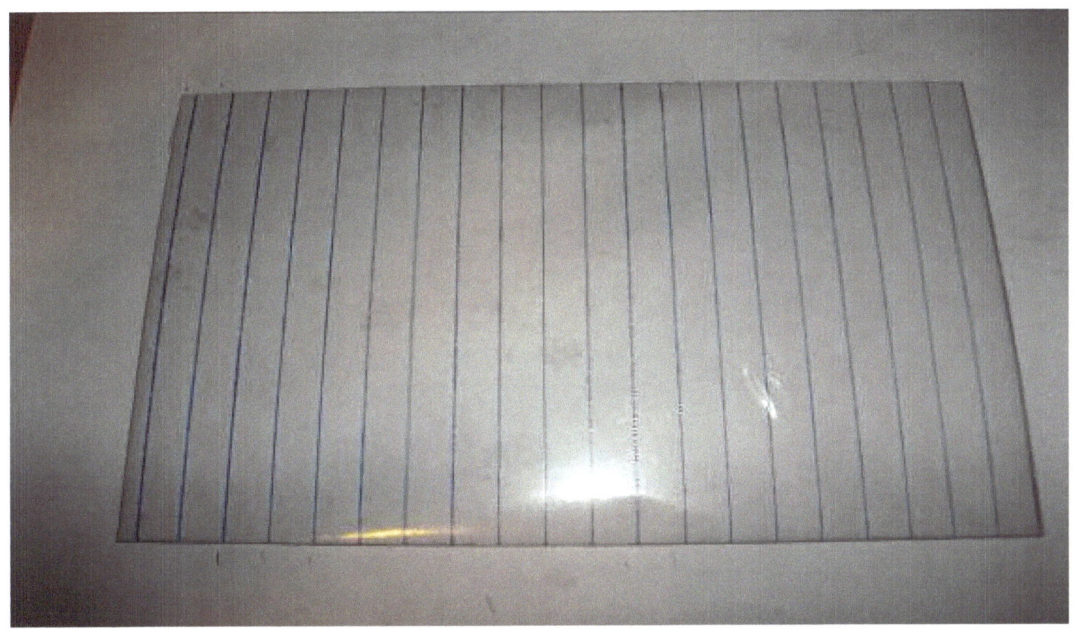

Place a sheet of notebook paper on the bottom edge of your cardboard holder aligning the notebook paper to find and mark the center most point of each row drawn on your card board holder.

Use the exact method to make your top marks on your cardboard holder.

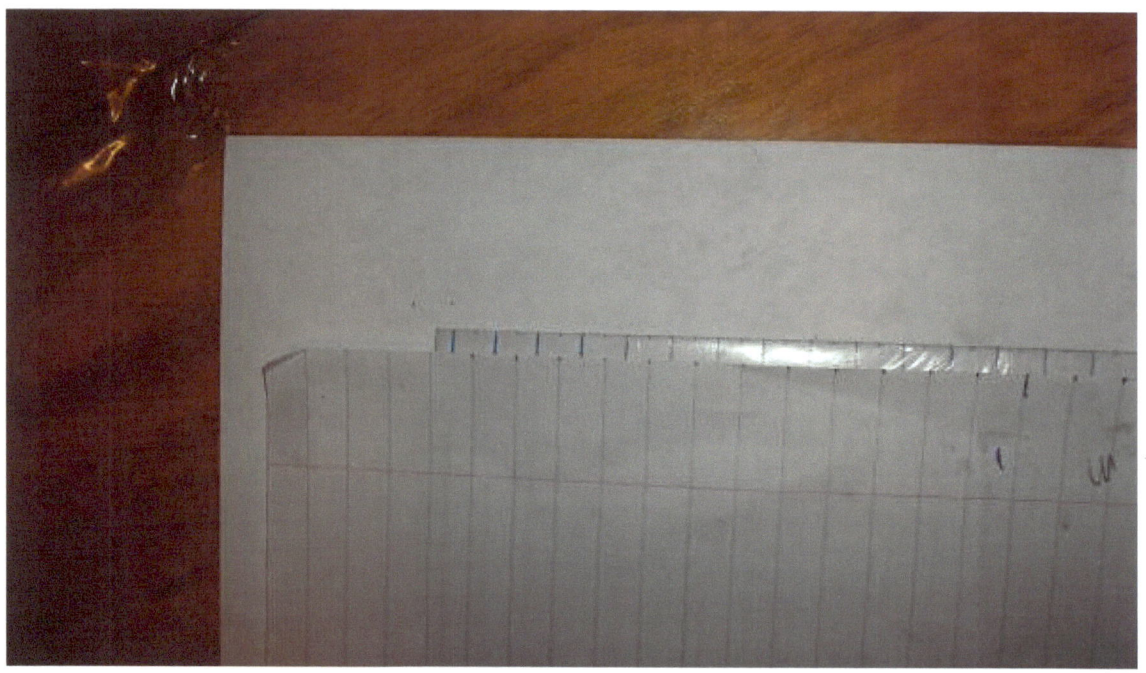

Using your ruler connect center marks of the row you just made.

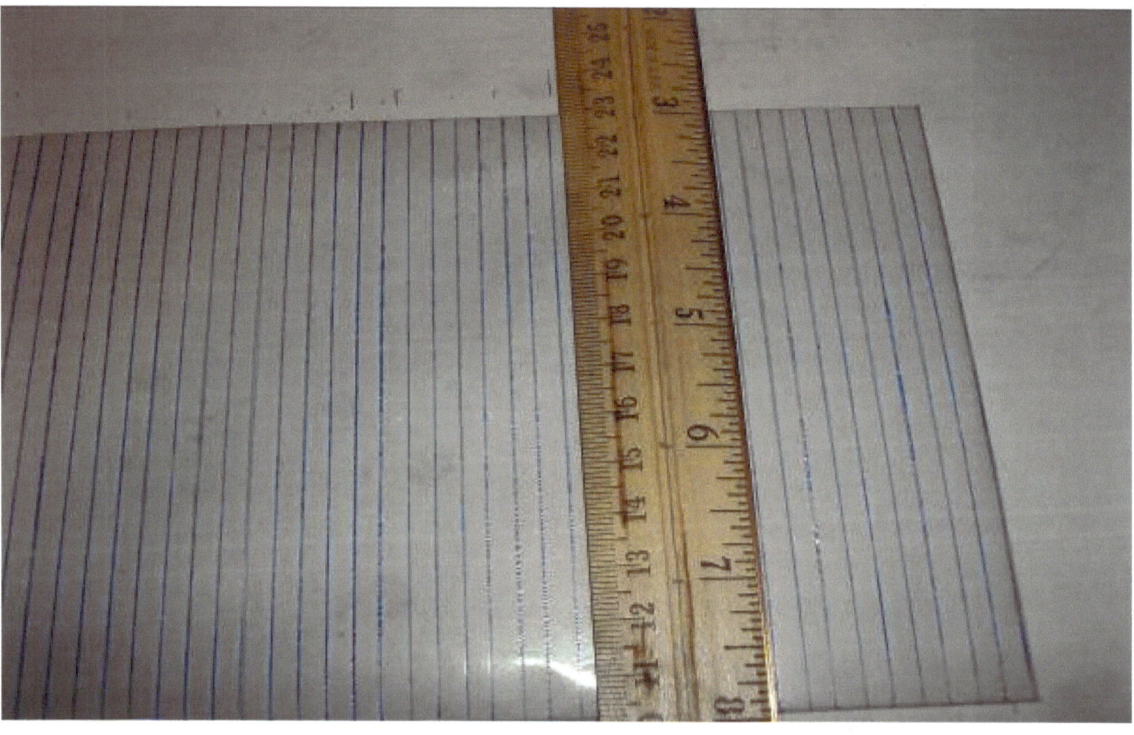

Using the same method you used to get the center marks on the bottom and top, you will now use the same method to get marks for the left and right side of the cardboard holder.

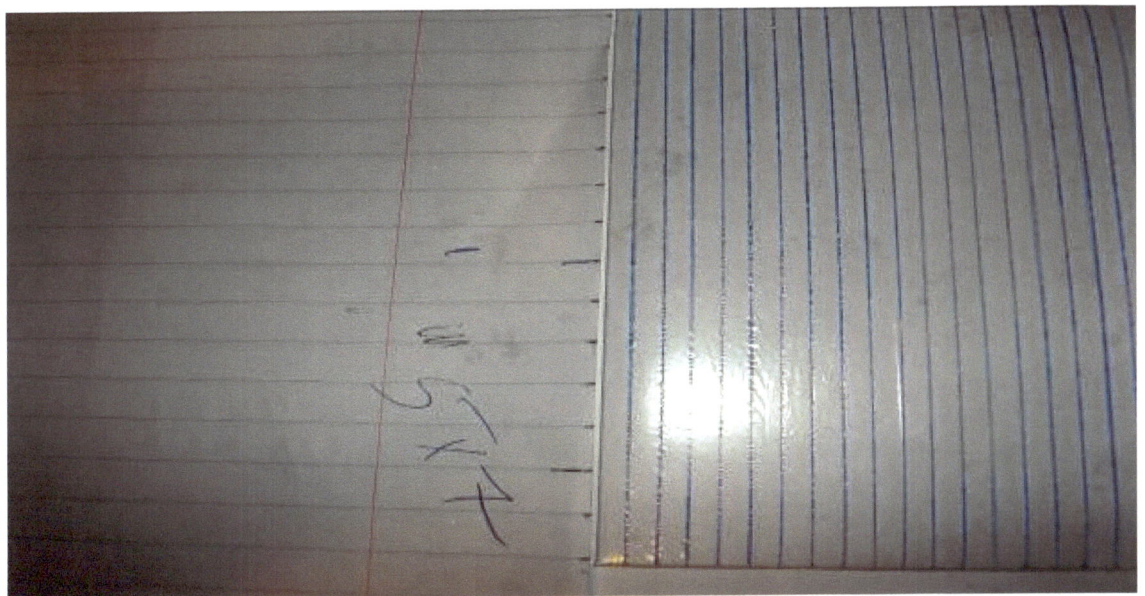

Remember to align your notebook paper with bottom edge aligned with a line of your notebook paper.

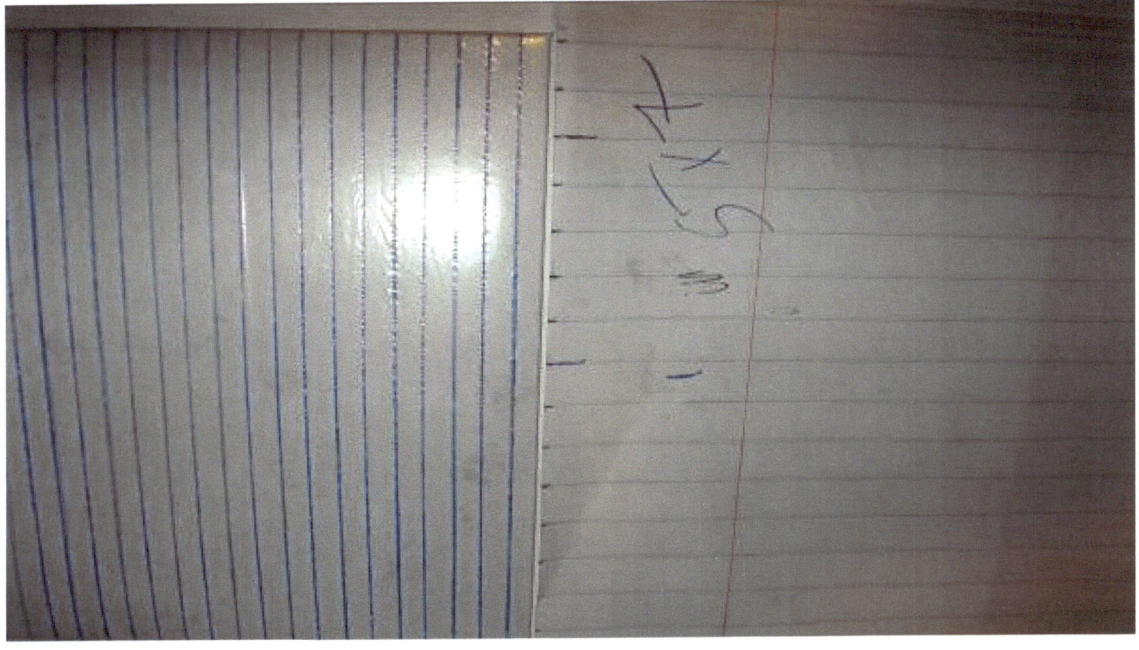

Draw lines connecting the marks using your ruler you just made form left to right.

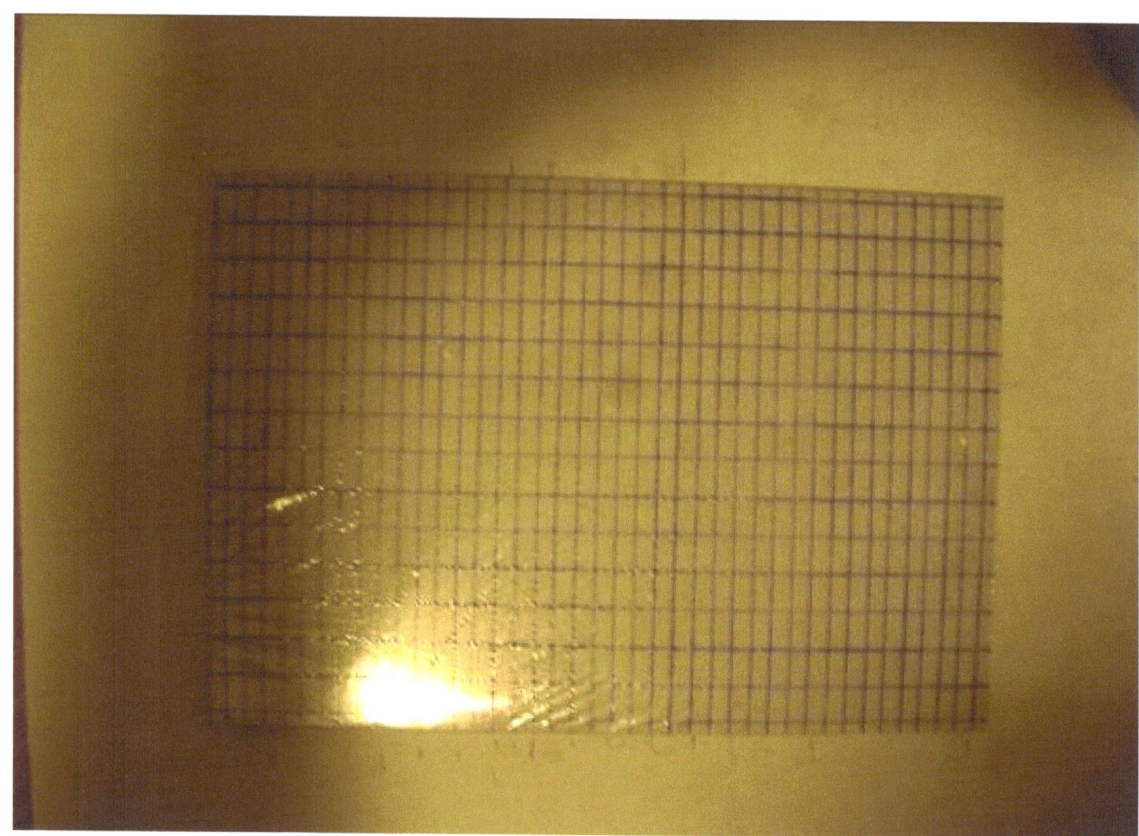

Once again align your notebook paper just as you did to find the center most point of each row you just constructed.

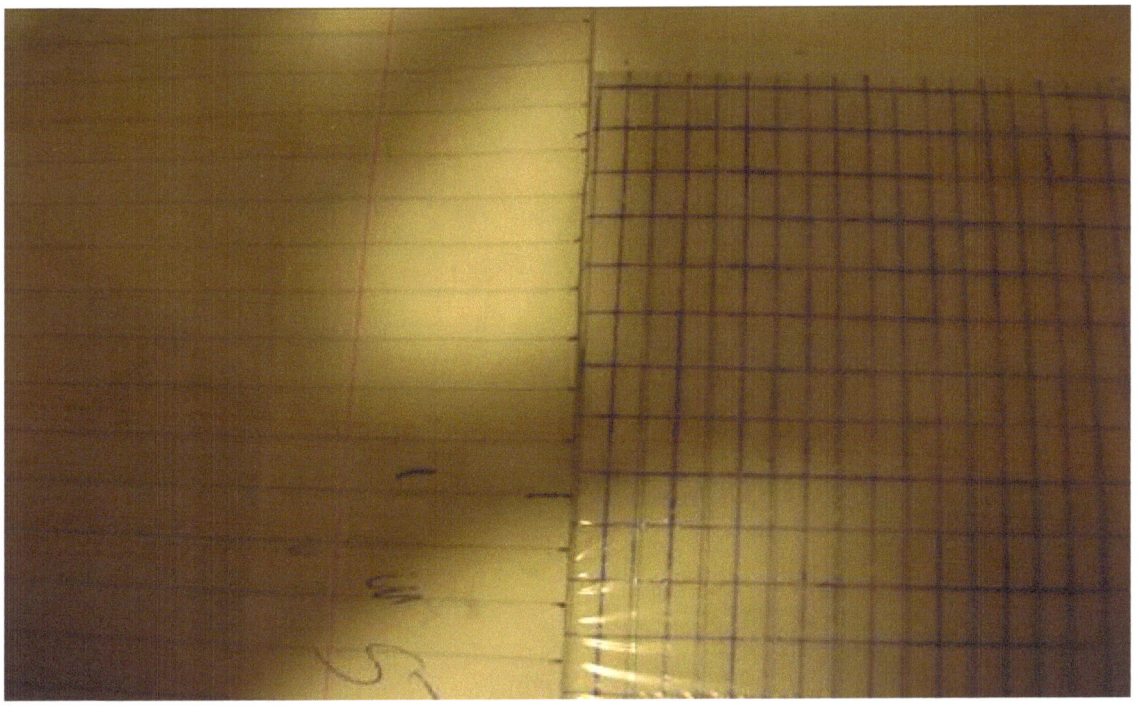

Making sure the right side is done in the same fashion.

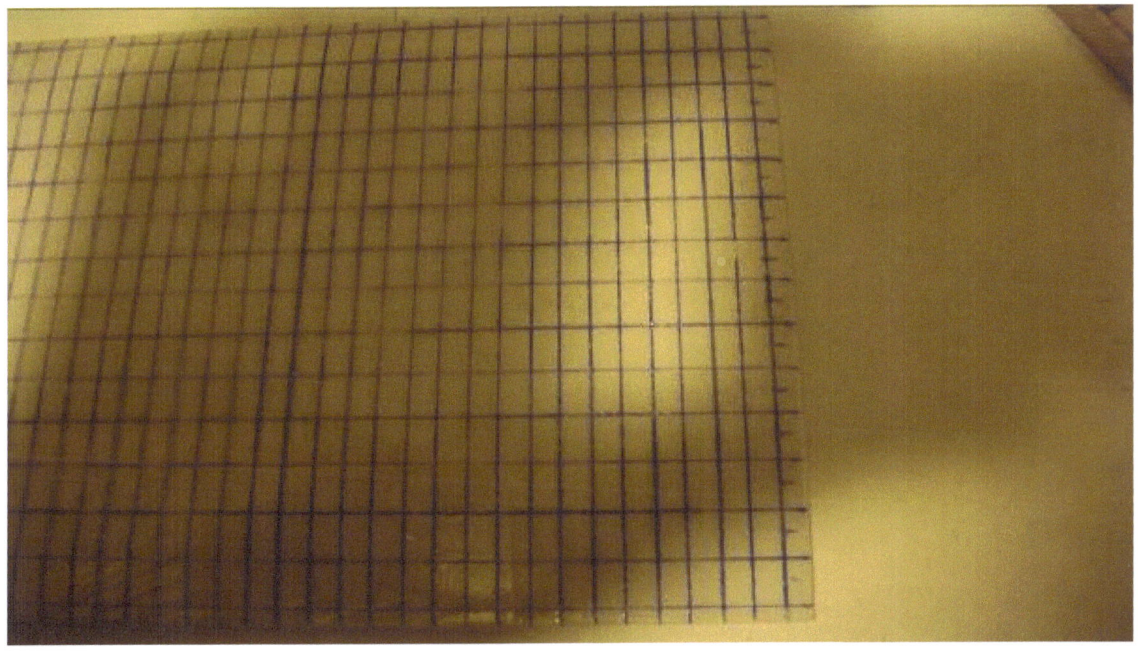

Using your ruler connect the center marks made on the left and right.

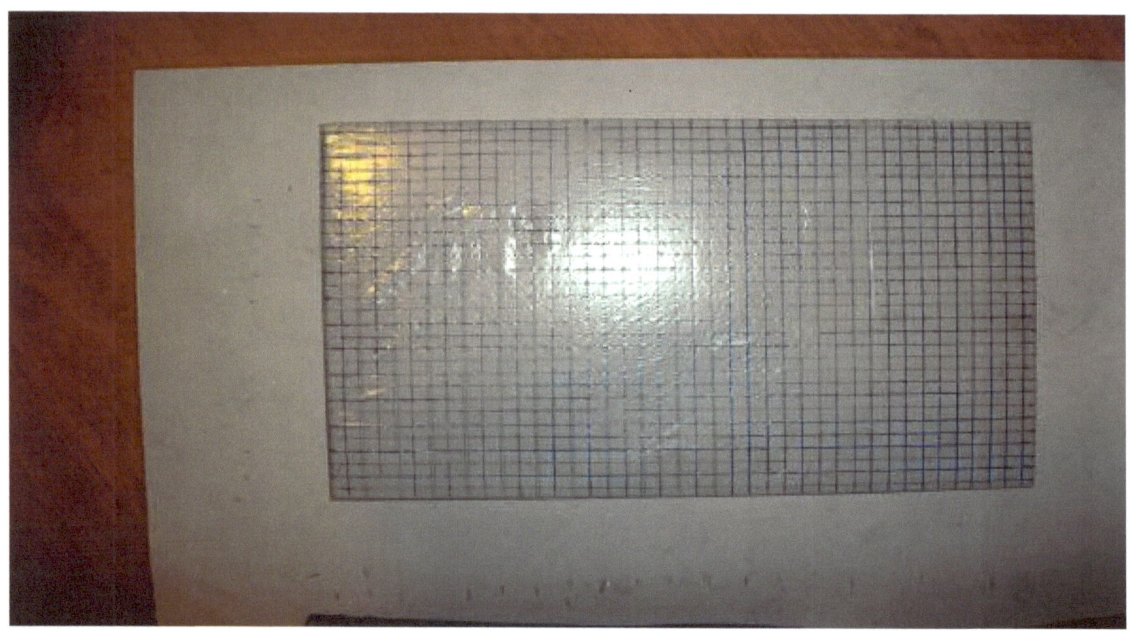

Carefully remove the plastic from around your cardboard holder.

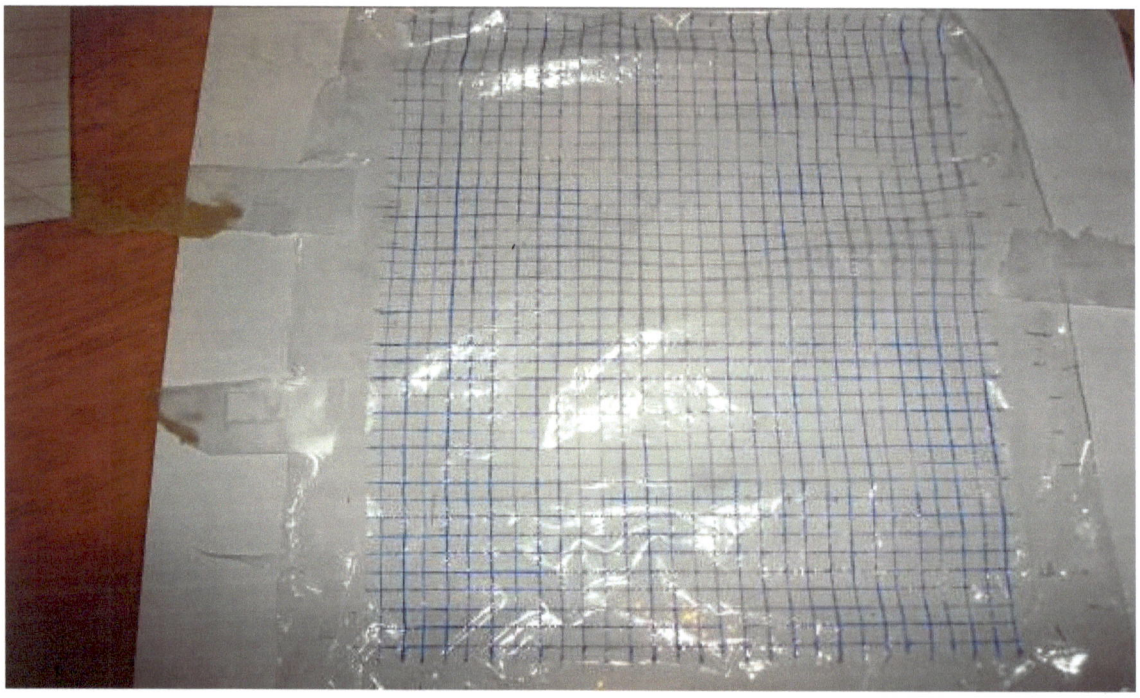

Turn over the ink drawn plastic cover with the ink side facing down toward your cardboard holder try to align as best as possible your ink drawn lines to match your cardboard paper lines.

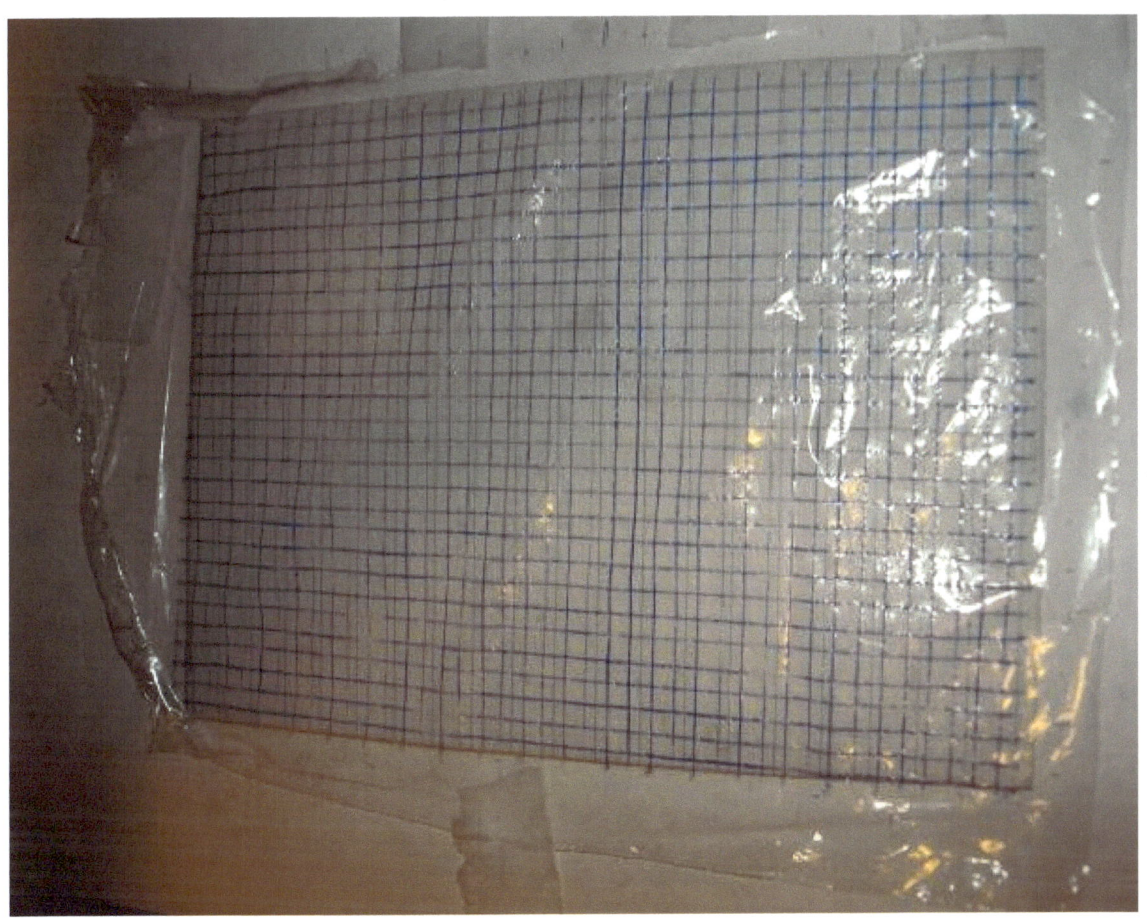

Turn over your cardboard picture holder and begin to tape the backside securely this time leaving the bottom end open. This is where you will insert your chosen drawn picture.

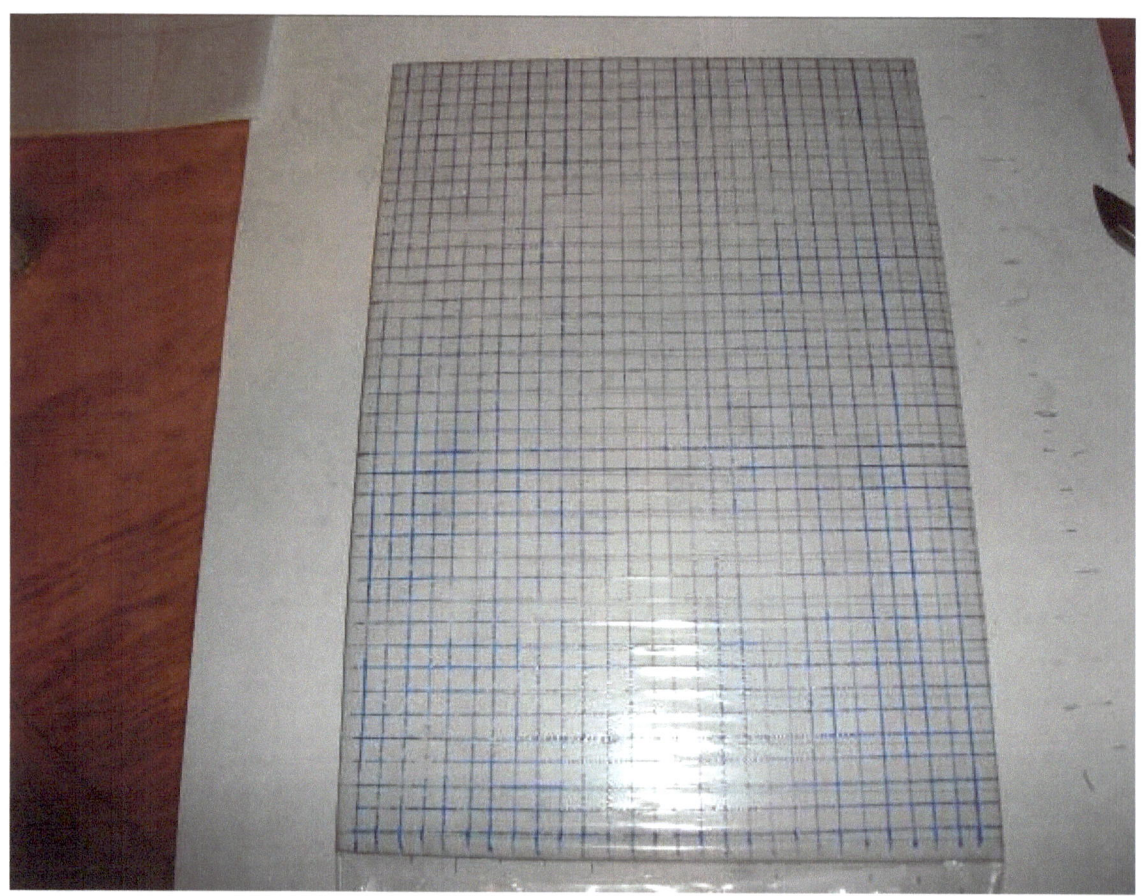

You are now finishing with the construction item 2, which will we call picture holder number 1.

Chapter 3- picture holder 2

You will again construct another picture holder only this time the blocks will be bigger. You will find that this picture holder will probably be used more often than the one with the smaller blocks. Using the same items as you used to construct the first picture holder. Scissors, tape, notebook paper, ink pen, plastic sandwich bag, ruler.

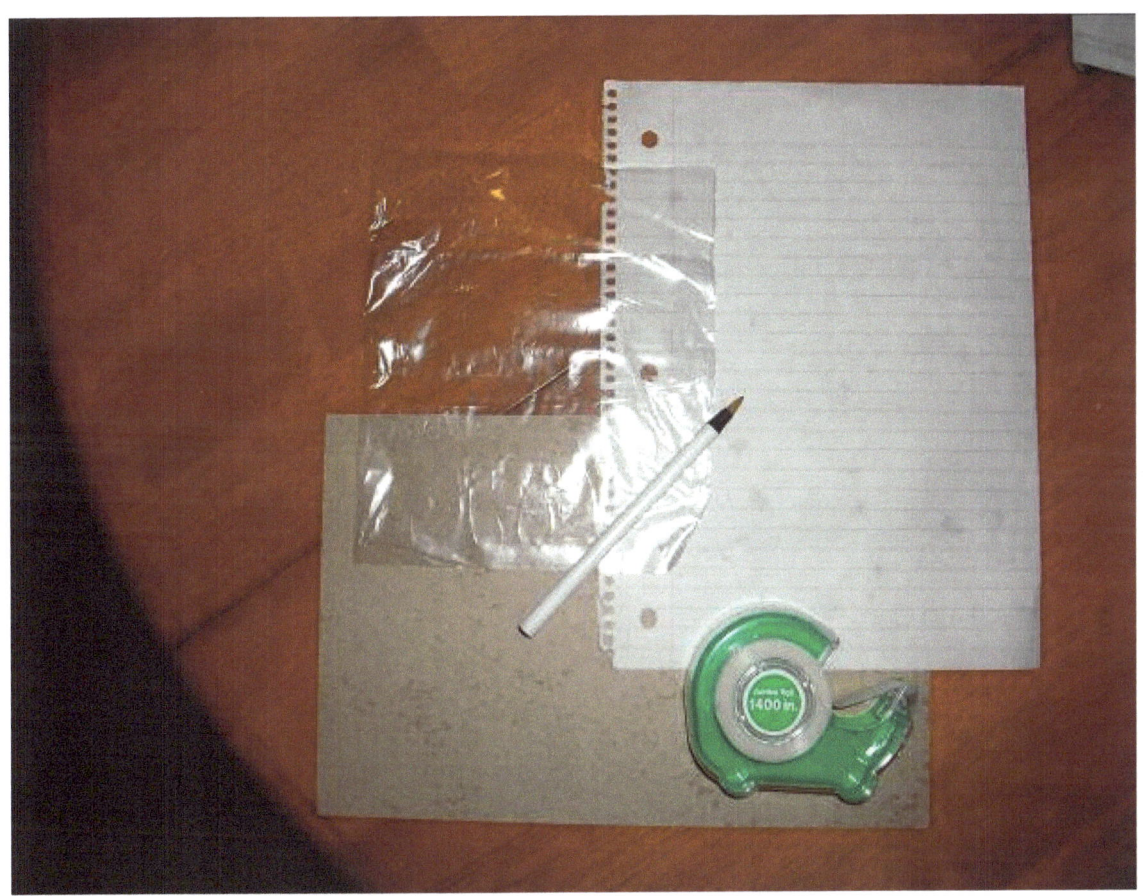

Using the remaining piece of cardboard used from the construction of the first two items. Cut a 5 by 7 piece. Place and align the outer edge of cardboard on the notebook paper.

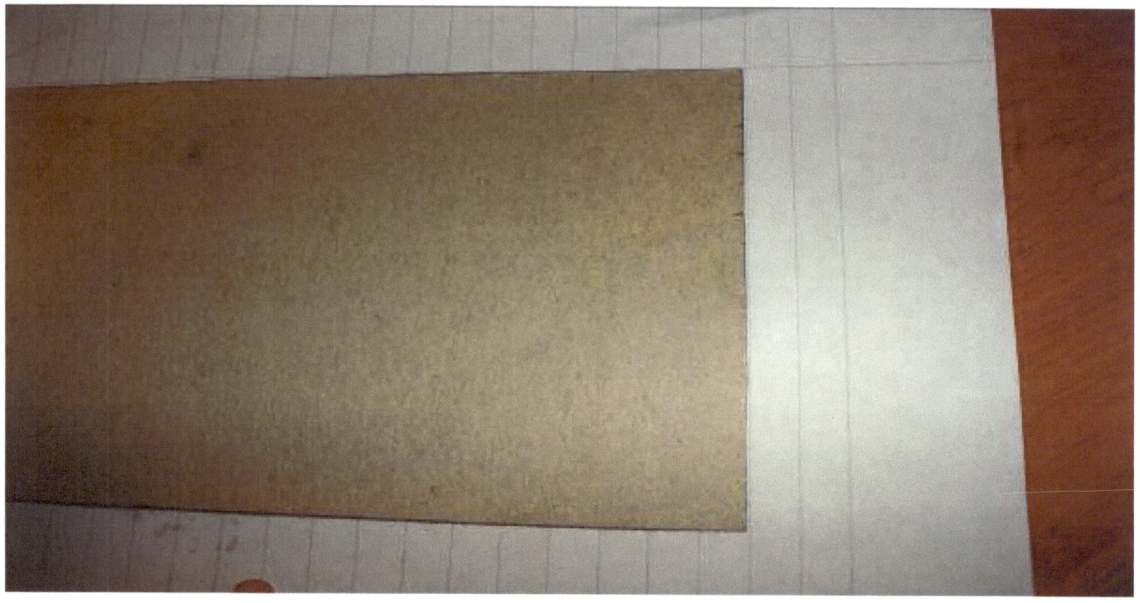

Fold the left and right side of paper around your cardboard just as you did with the first picture holder. Remember to tape each side.

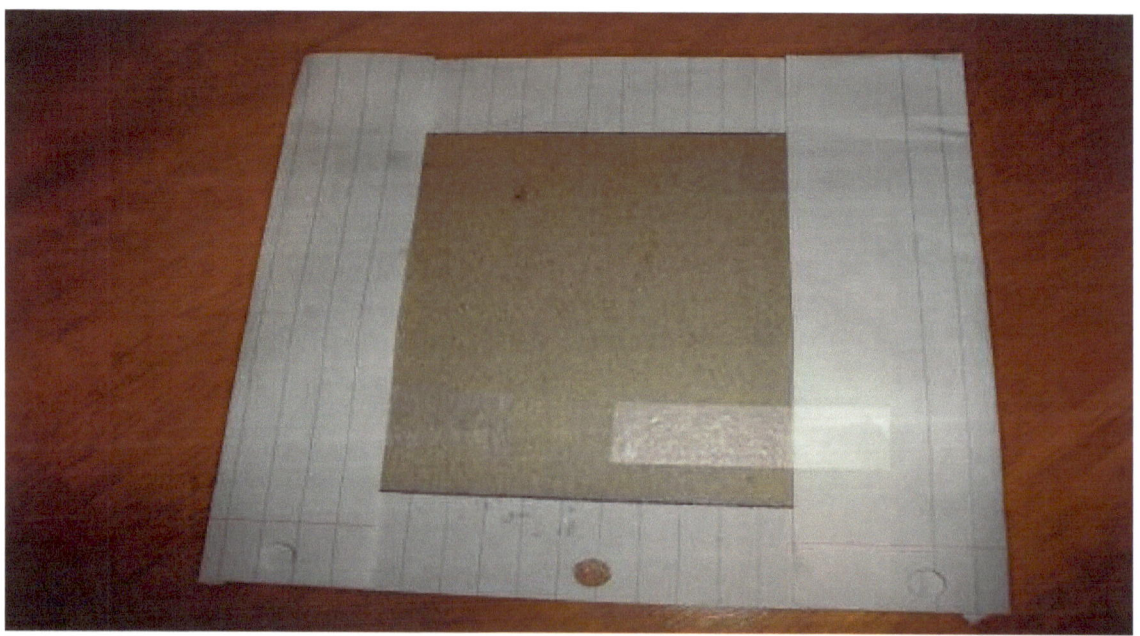

Tape the top and bottom.

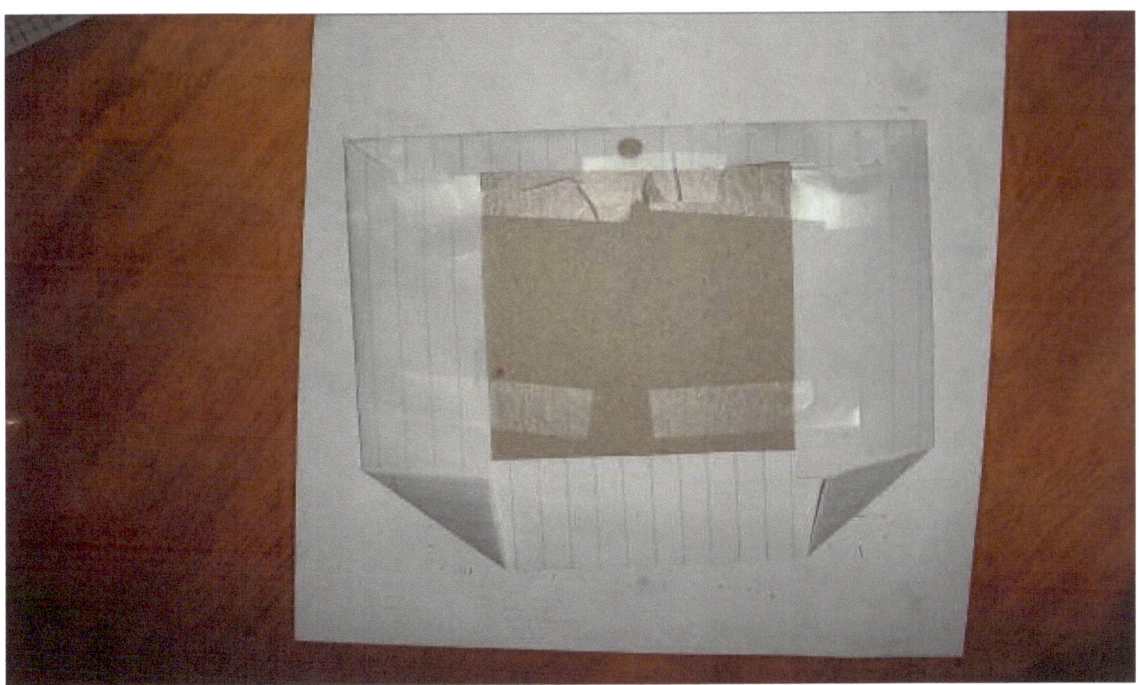

Turn over your cardboard holder with the lined paper side facing upward.

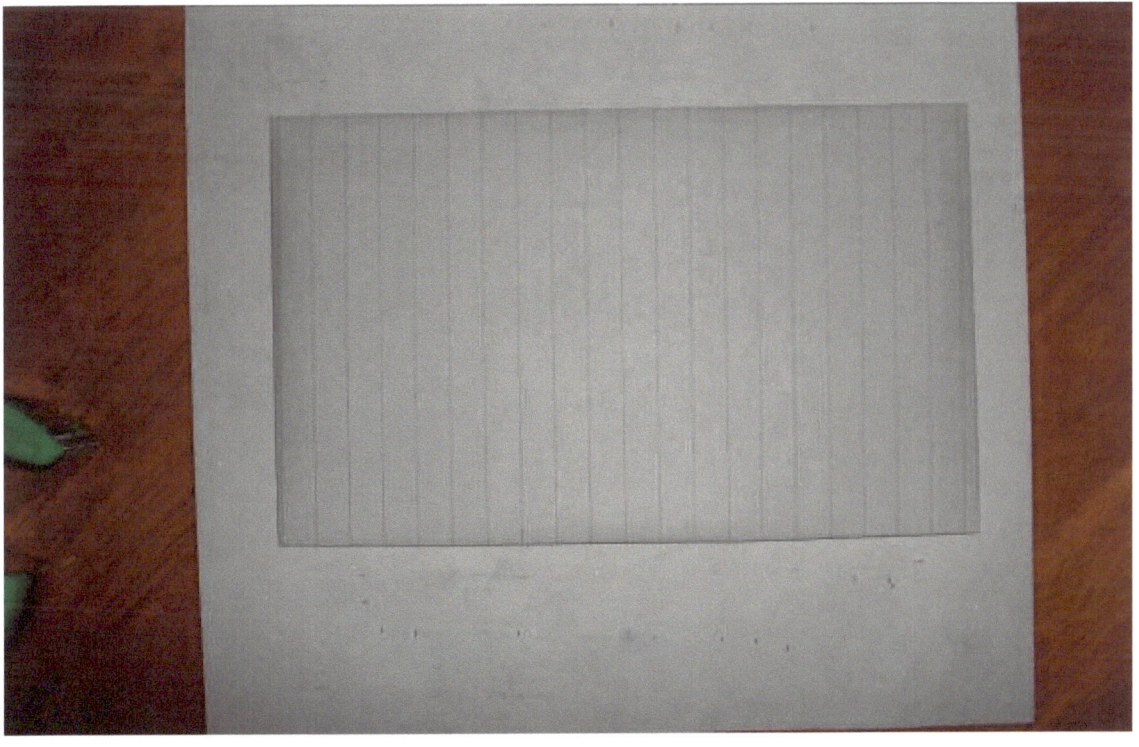

Place your plastic cover over the cardboard papered holder.

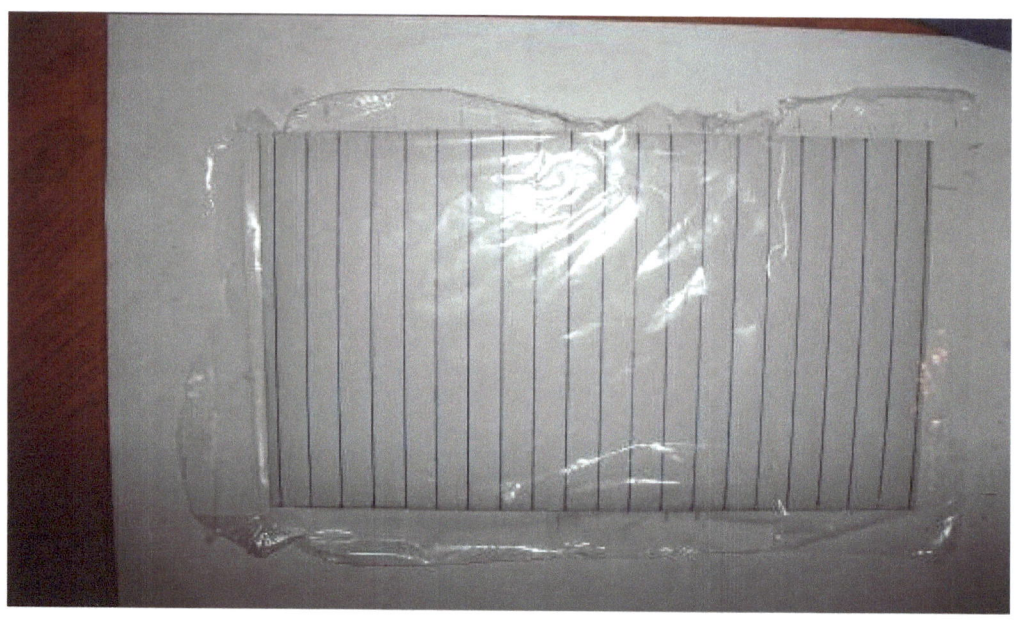

Turn over your picture holder and begin to tape your plastic cover around the holder. Remember to not tape securely. You will remove the plastic soon. Draw lines matching the exact lines on the holder.

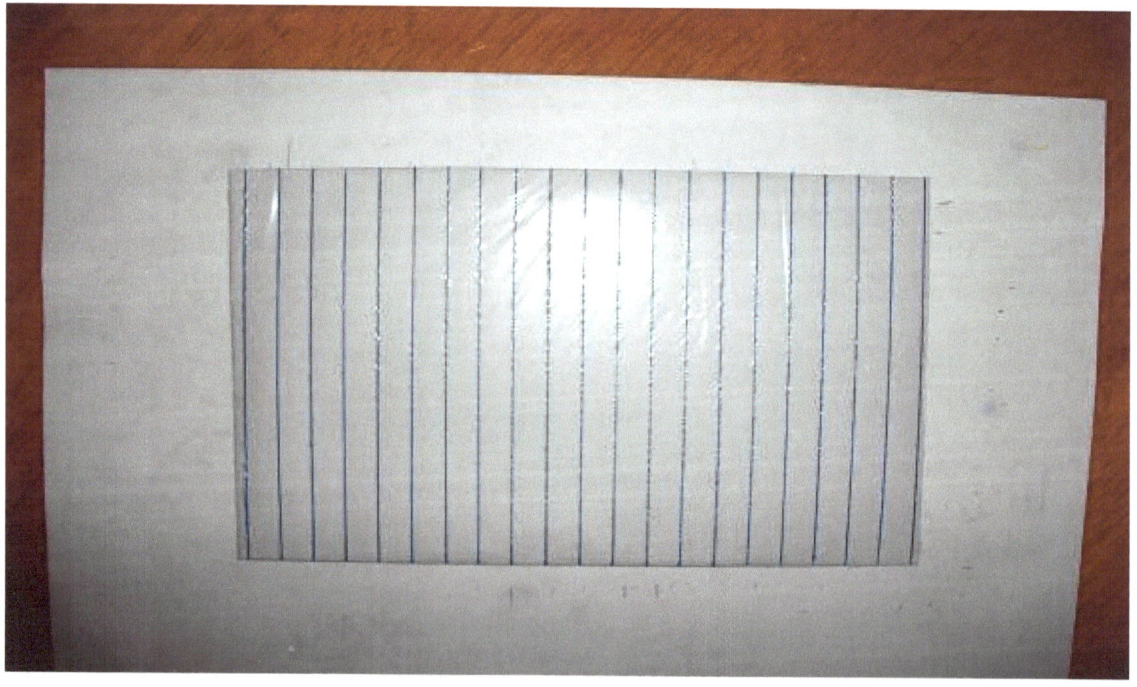

You will now draw lines from left to right using the same method to mark your lines you used constructing picture holder 1. Place and align you notebook paper with outer edge of your picture holder. Making sure the bottom most edge of your picture holder is aligned with your notebook paper.

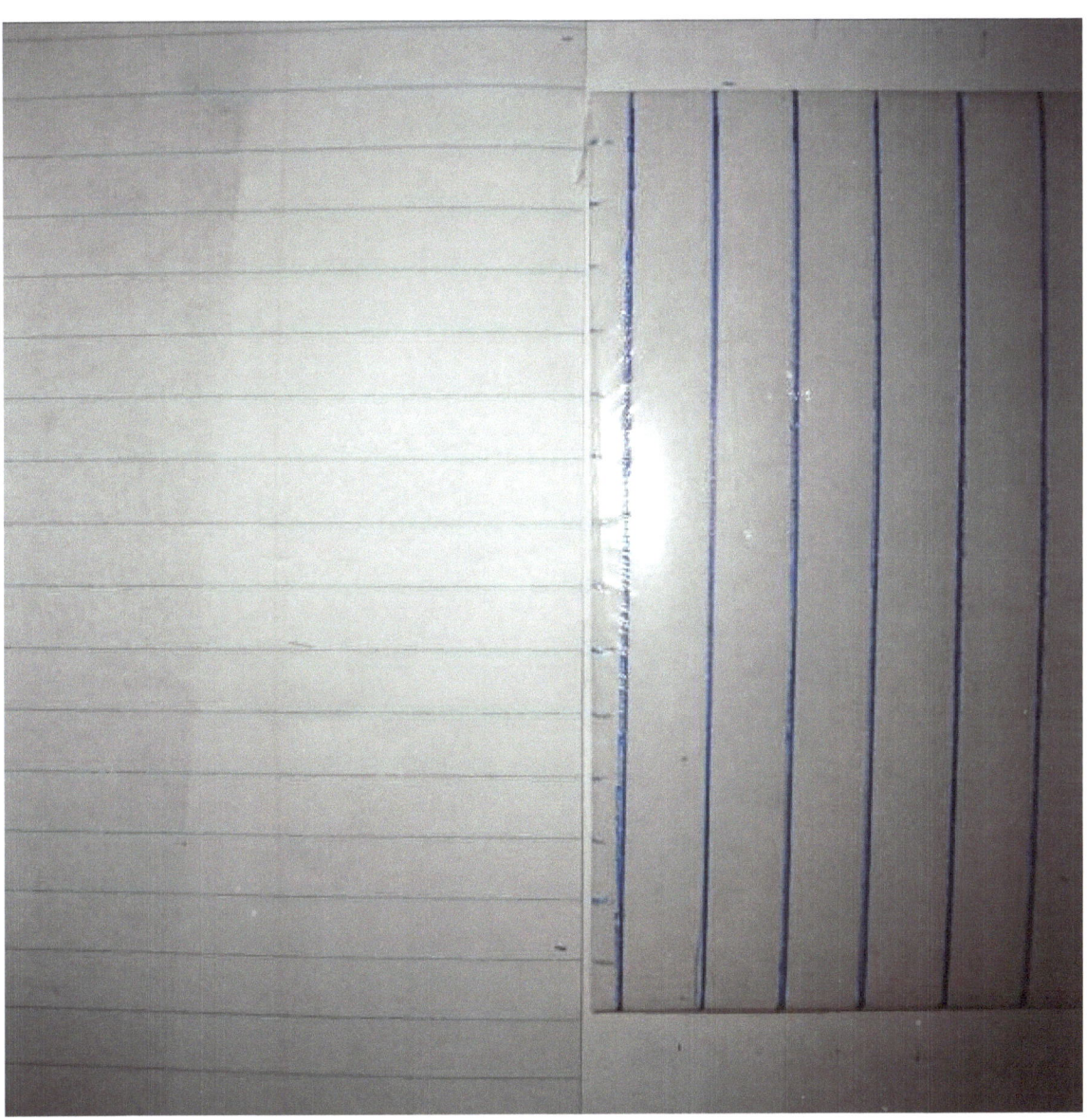

Make sure you keep the same method you used on the left to get your marks on the right side.

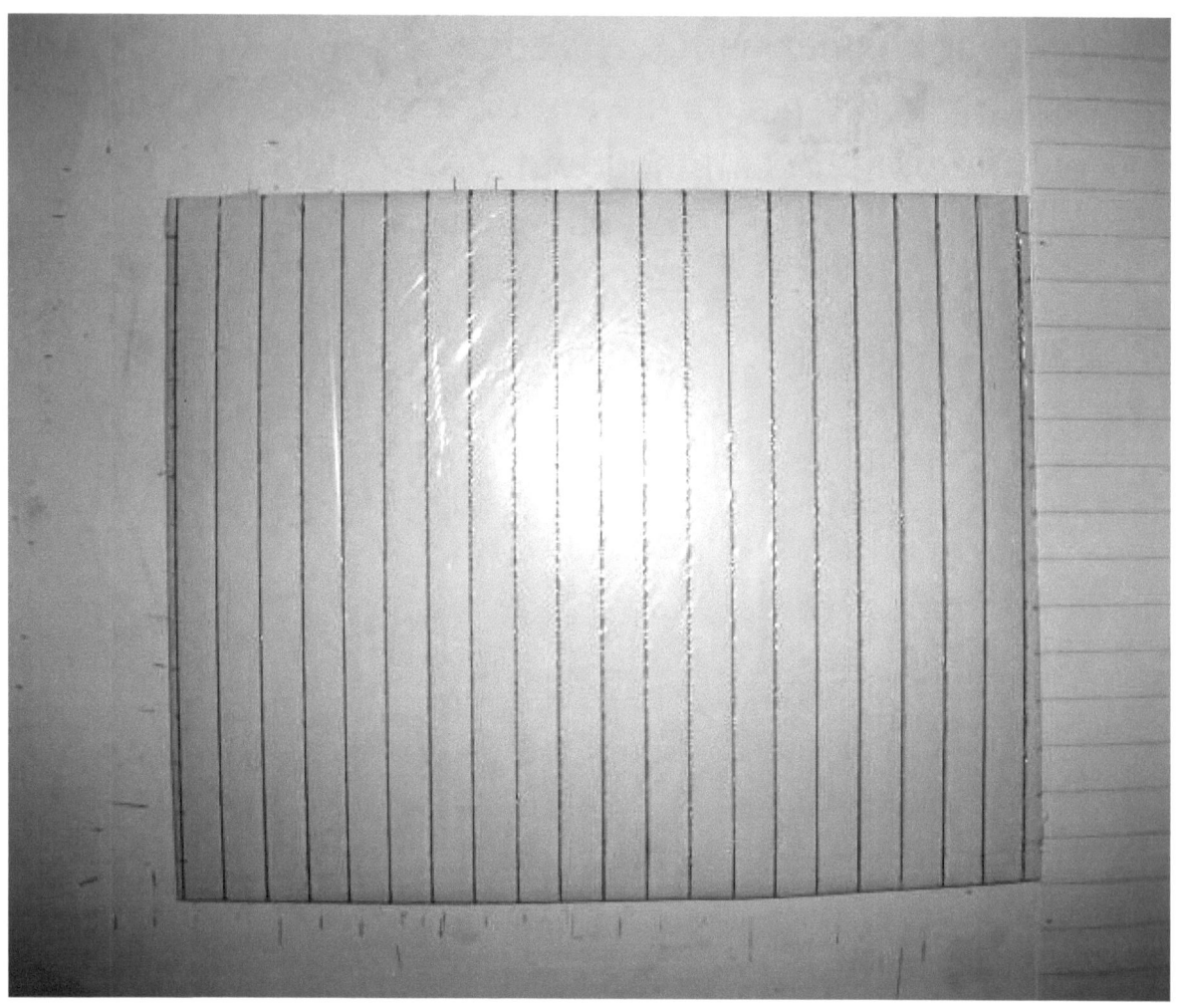

Using your ruler connect the marks you made on the left and right side.

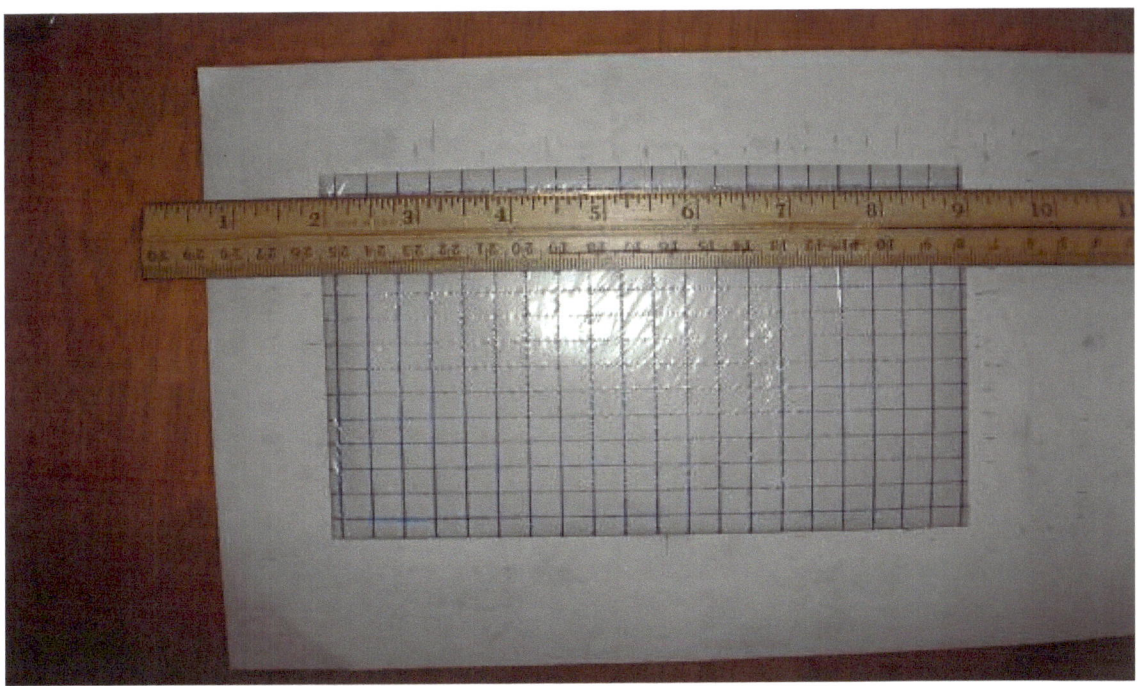

When done connecting your marks your second picture holder should resemble the one below.

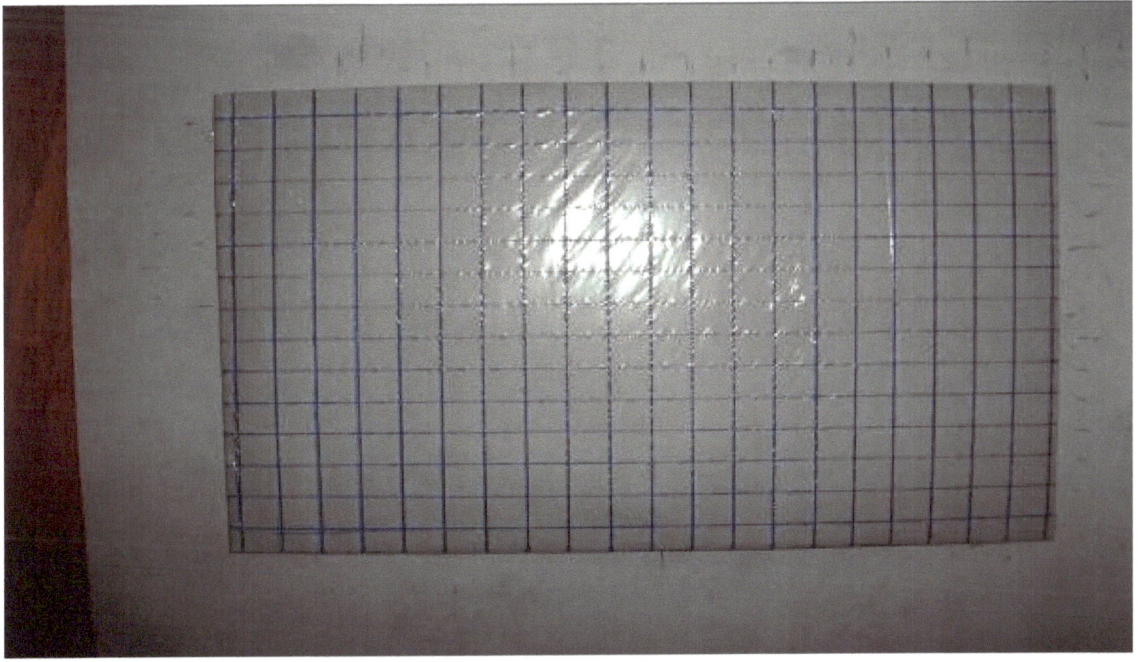

Turn over your picture and carefully remove the plastic covering.

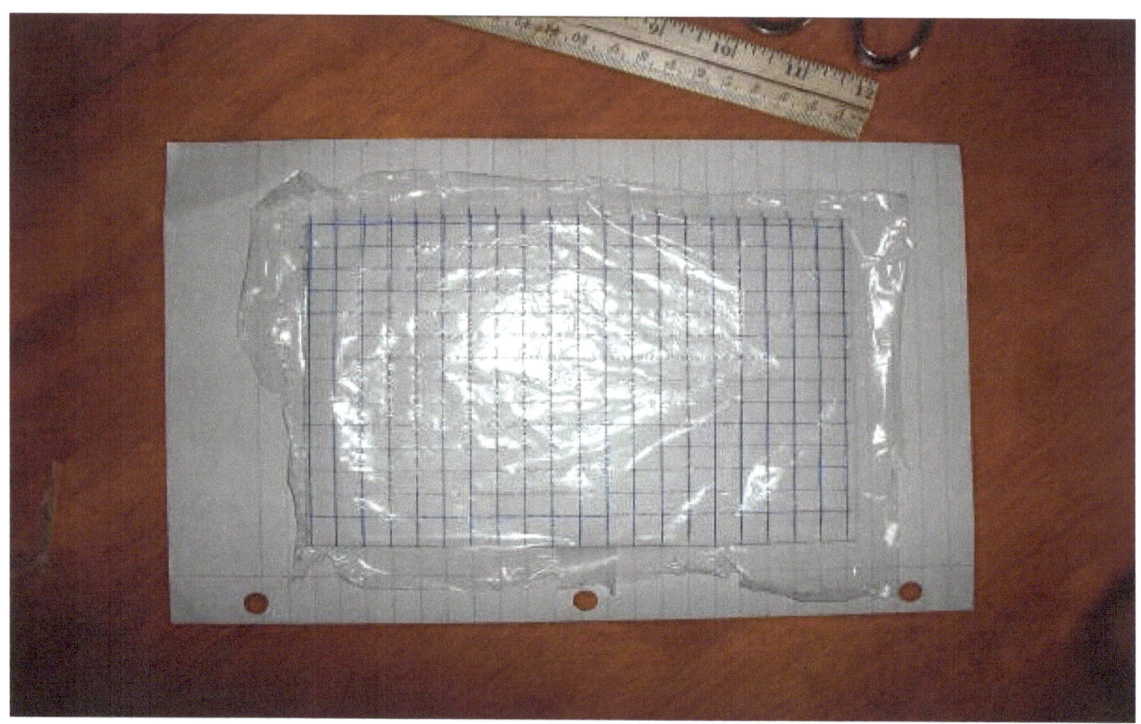

Place the ink drawn side of the plastic towards the lined side of your holder.

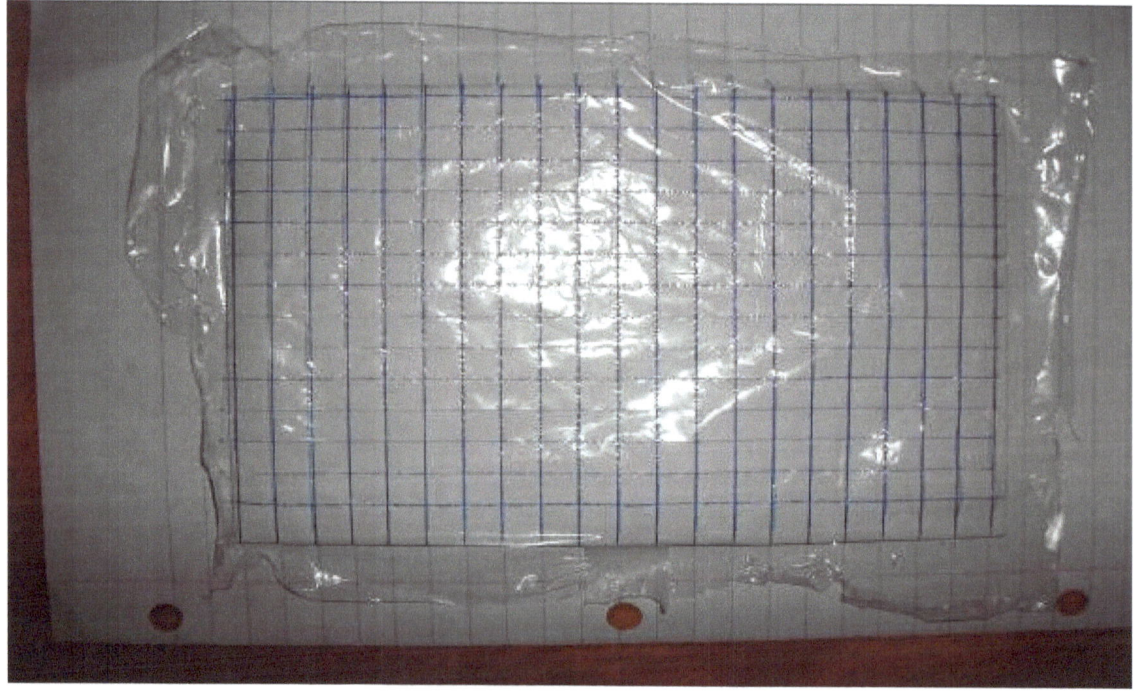

Turn over your picture holder, carefully and securely tape the backside of your picture holder, this time taping it securely, leaving one end left or right open to insert a picture into. Remember to try and align as best as possible your ink drawn lines with the lines on your picture holder.

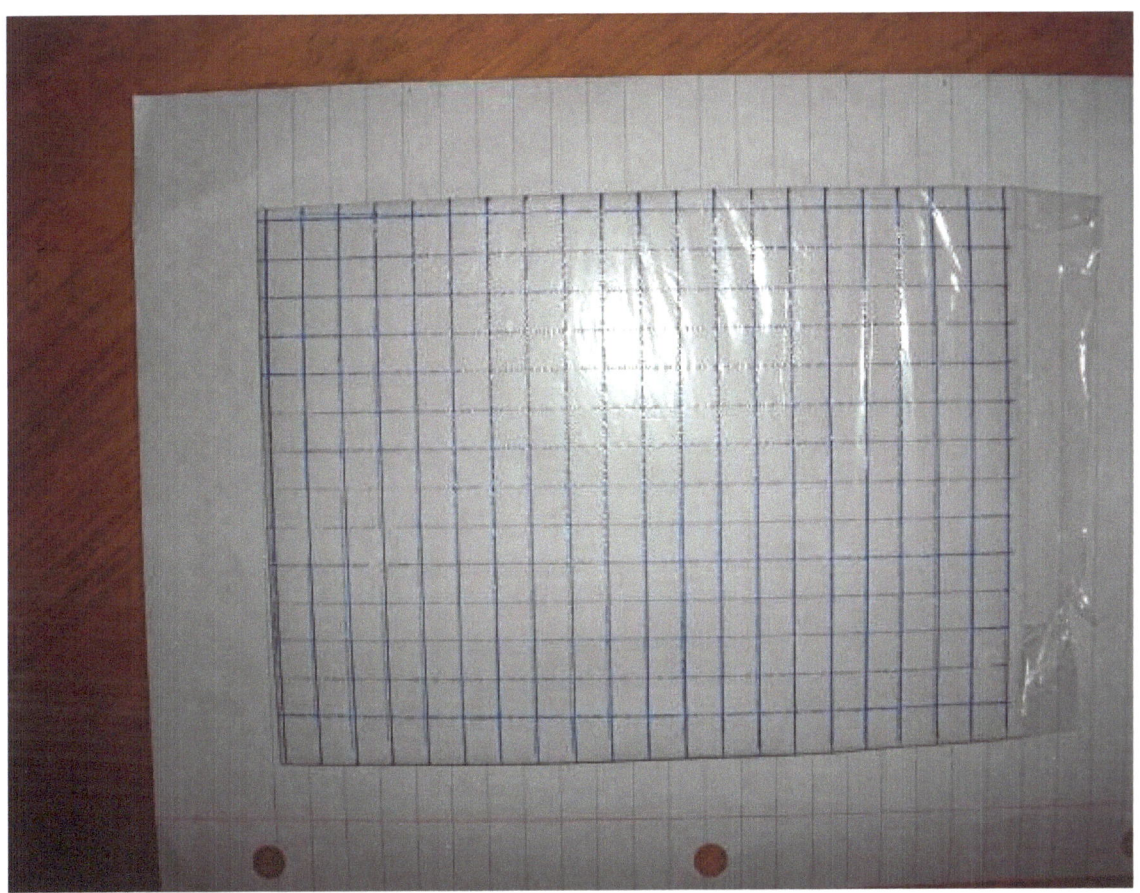

You have completed the construction of item number 3.
Picture holder 2.

Chapter 4 – using constructed items

These are the three items you will be using to draw and enhance any picture 5 by 7 or smaller.

Picture holder 1 with the smaller blocks.
Picture holder 2 with the larger blocks.
Enlargement ruler

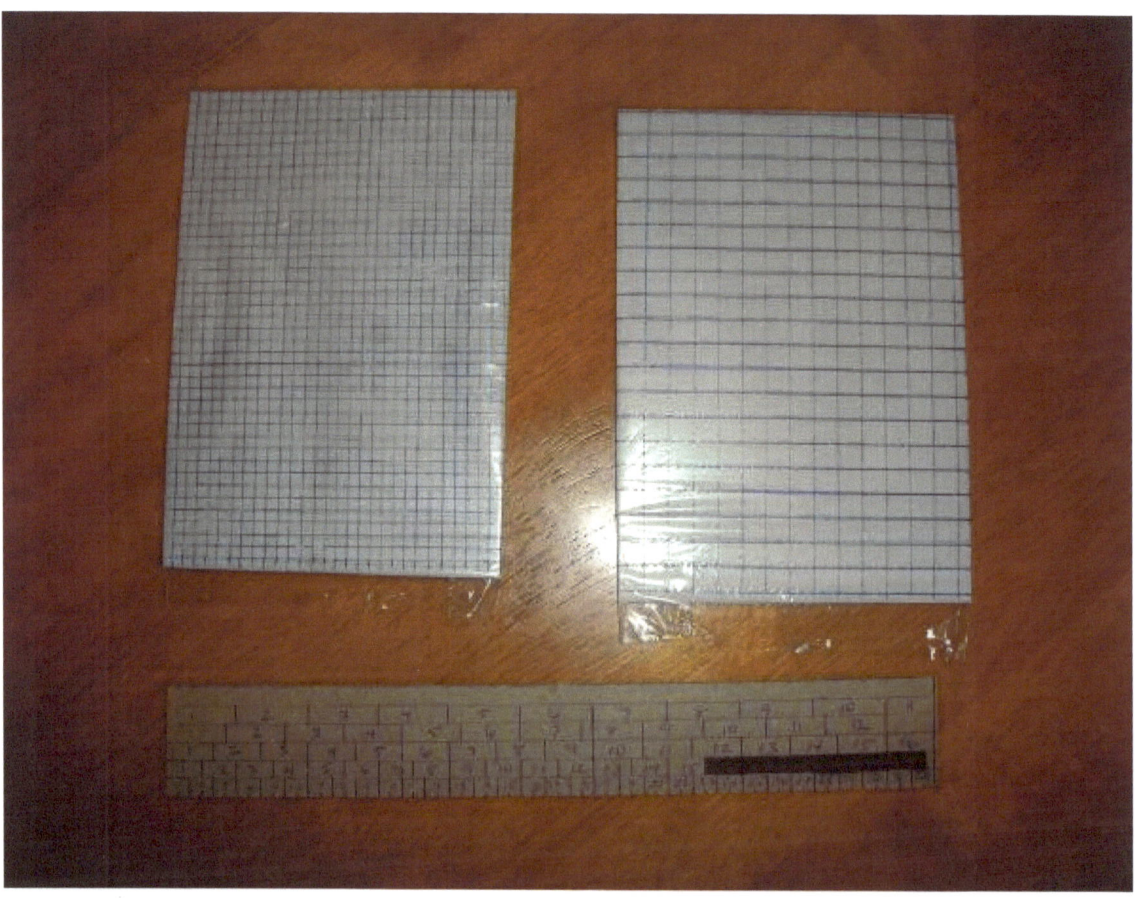

You will see the value in the items you have constructed in the next chapter.

Our next step will be to choose a picture you wish to draw close to the one I have selected.

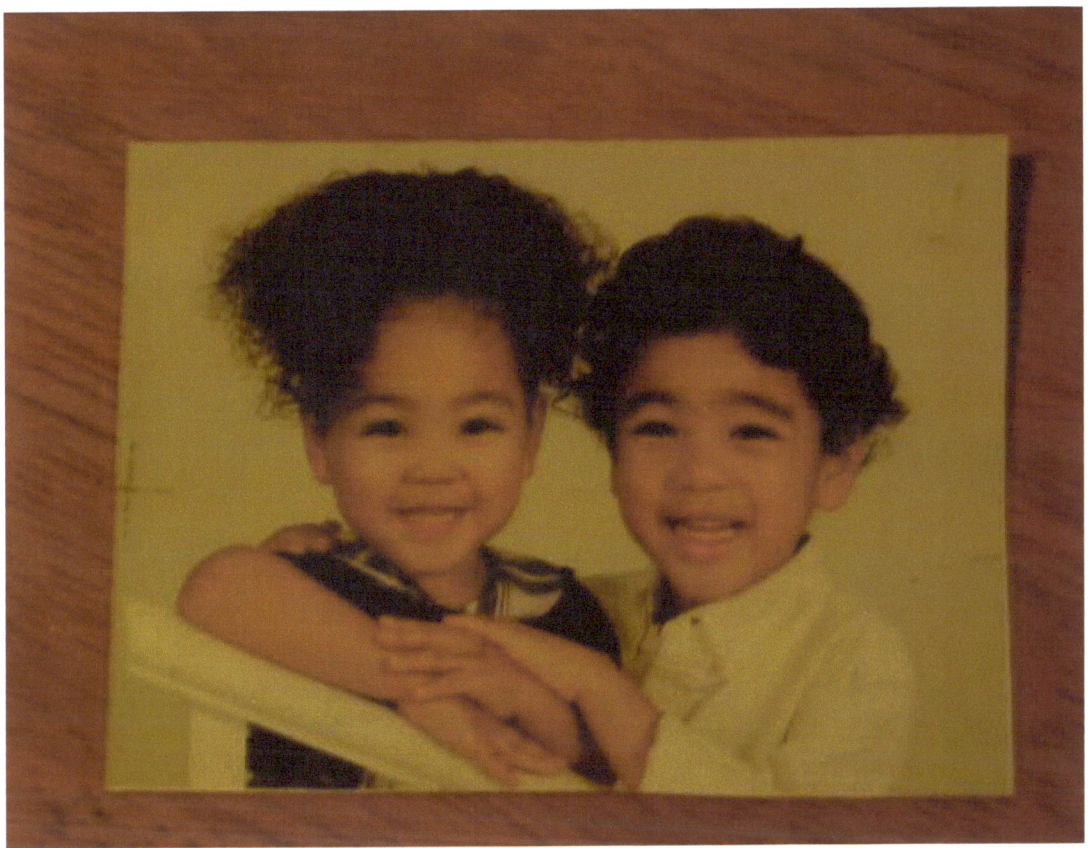

we will now need two sheets of printer paper (advanced artists know to get one of printer paper and the other drawing paper). As for me I prefer the first (printer paper).

Your newly constructed cardboard ruler, both picture holders, drawing pencils, and scissors.

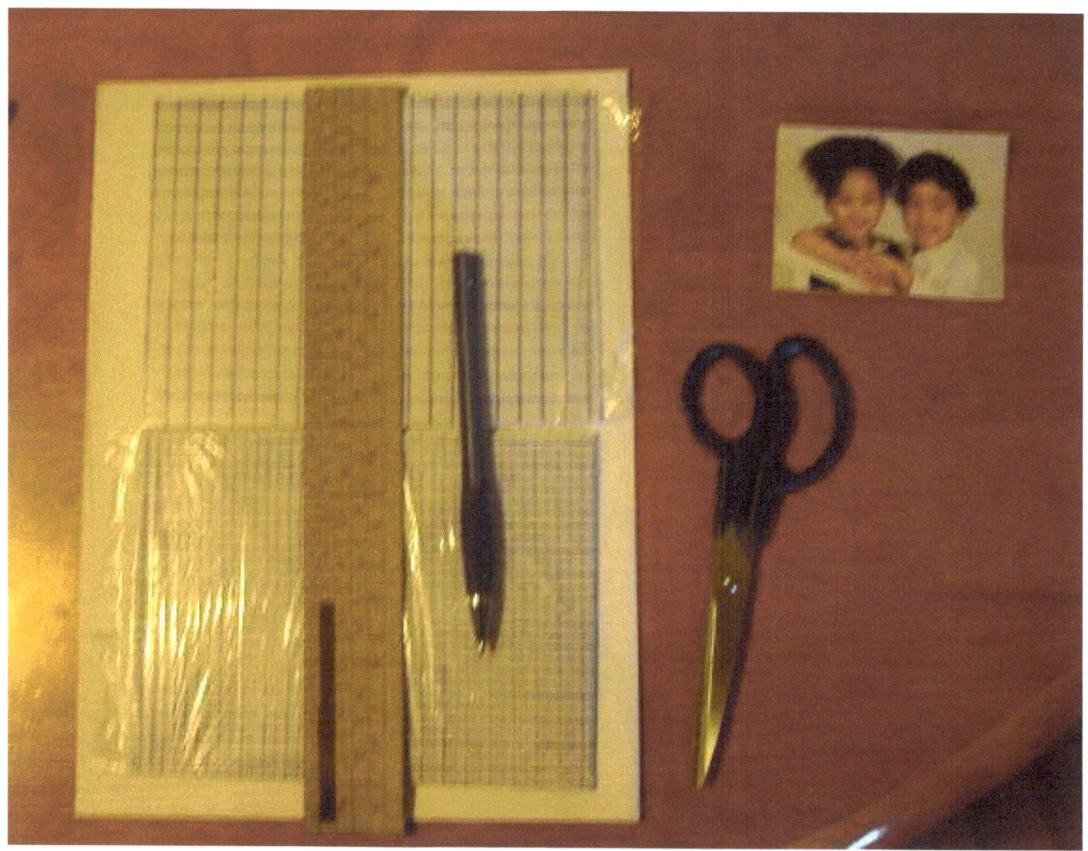

Next we must decide which picture holder to use; we do this by placing your chosen picture into the first (holder with the smallest blocks) of the two picture holders you constructed.

Place the picture you chose to draw inside the
picture holder. Try to align the outer edge of picture
with the drawn ink lines of your picture holder.

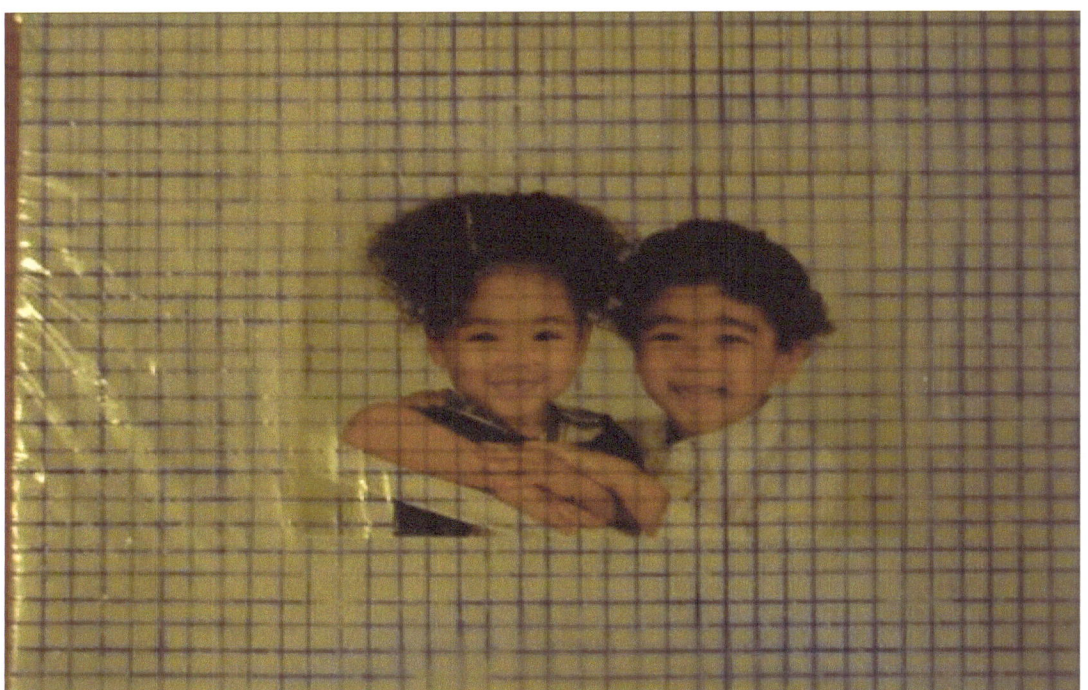

We will now count the blocks that cover the facial part of the chosen portrait, both vertical (up or down) and horizontal. This will help you to decide which row you will use on your cardboard ruler as well as which picture holder will be the best to use.

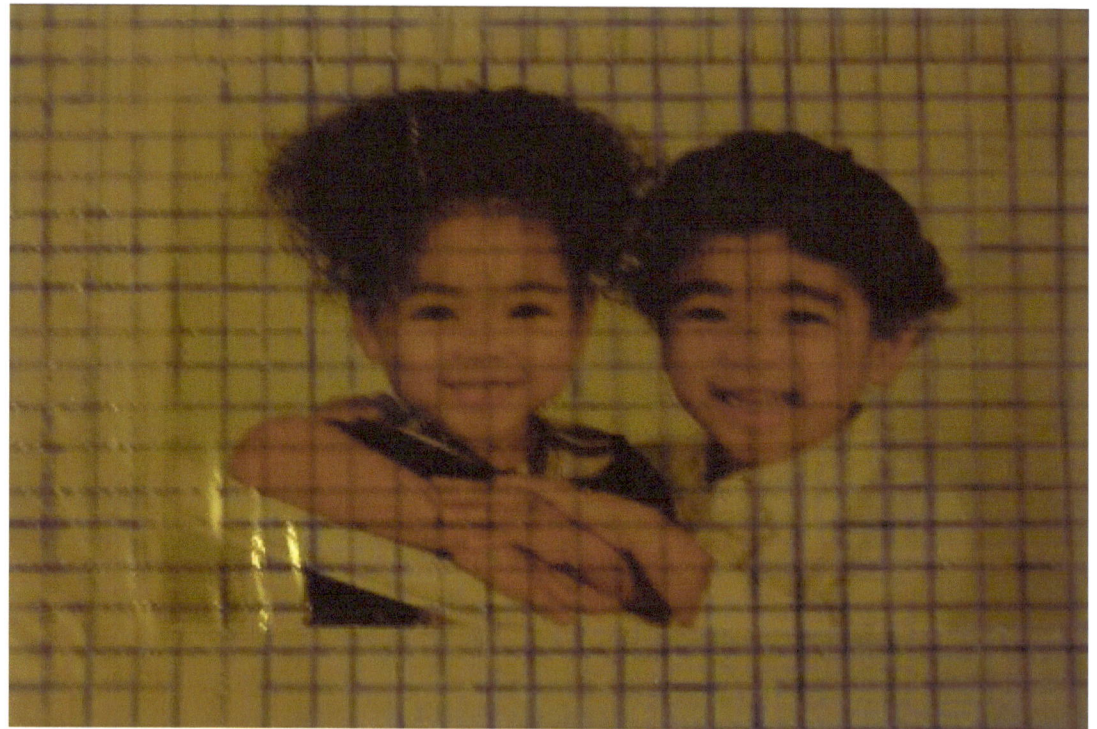

My chosen picture is inserted into the picture holder with the smaller blocks. (17 by 15 - counting blocks in the picture vertical and horizontal) Looking at your ruler row 3 is the only row with 16 blocks horizontal, when looking at the vertical blocks there are 15 blocks needed to draw the picture with this holder using row 3 on your cardboard ruler (your will need bigger paper to draw this picture using the smaller block picture holder) since we are using regular printer paper looking at your card board ruler your paper can only hold 12 blocks vertically on row 3.

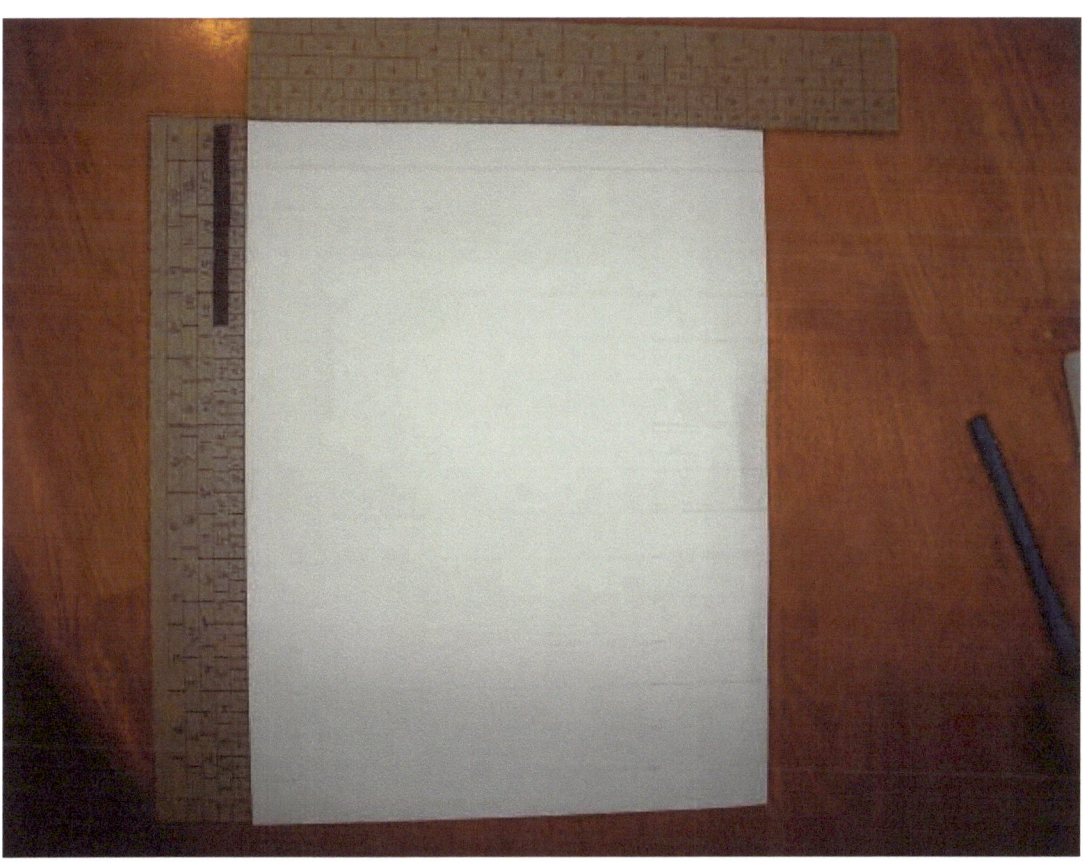

Now we try the second picture holder (the one with the larger blocks) repeating the same steps as we did with the first picture holder. Remember to align the outer edge of your picture with the drawn lines of the picture holder.

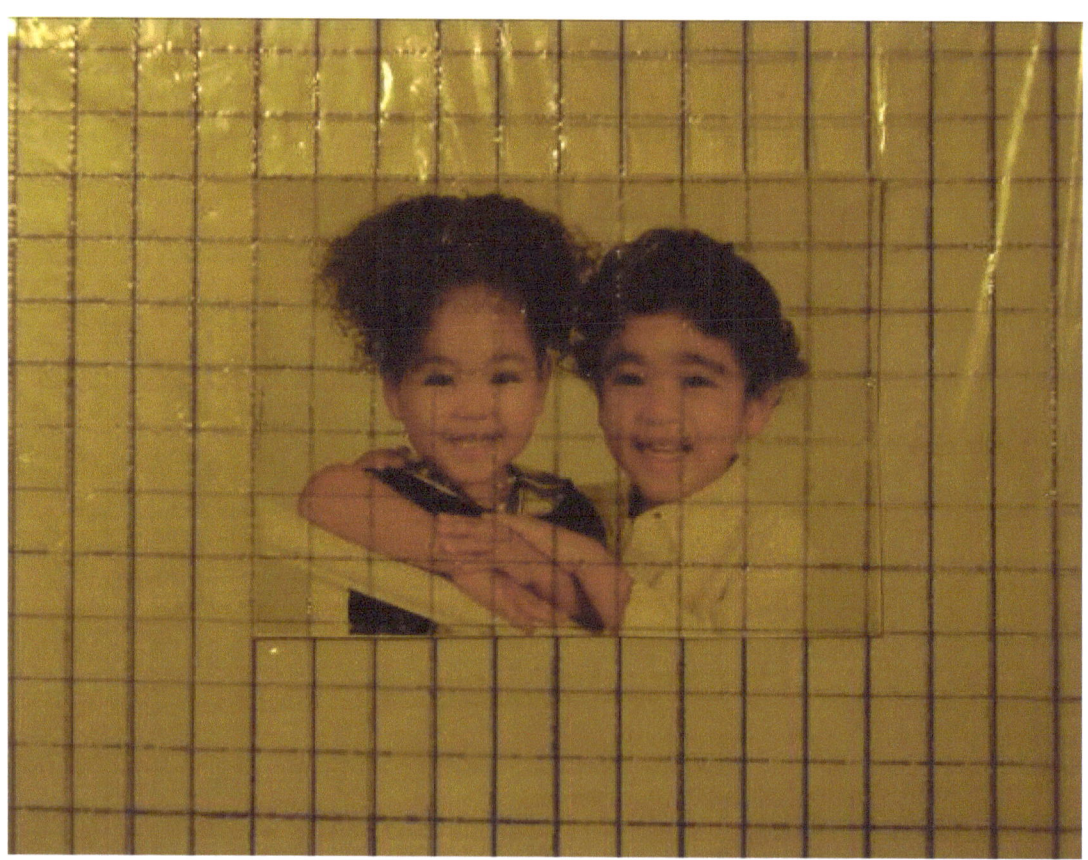

Chapter 5 – setting up your paper

I have decided that the second picture holder will be the one I use to demonstrate the simple technique of how to draw quality portraits. This picture holder (larger blocks) is 9 by 7. Looking at my cardboard ruler, I can use rows 3, 4, and 5. This is the enlargement and centering process, to bring balance to your picture. I choose to use row 3.

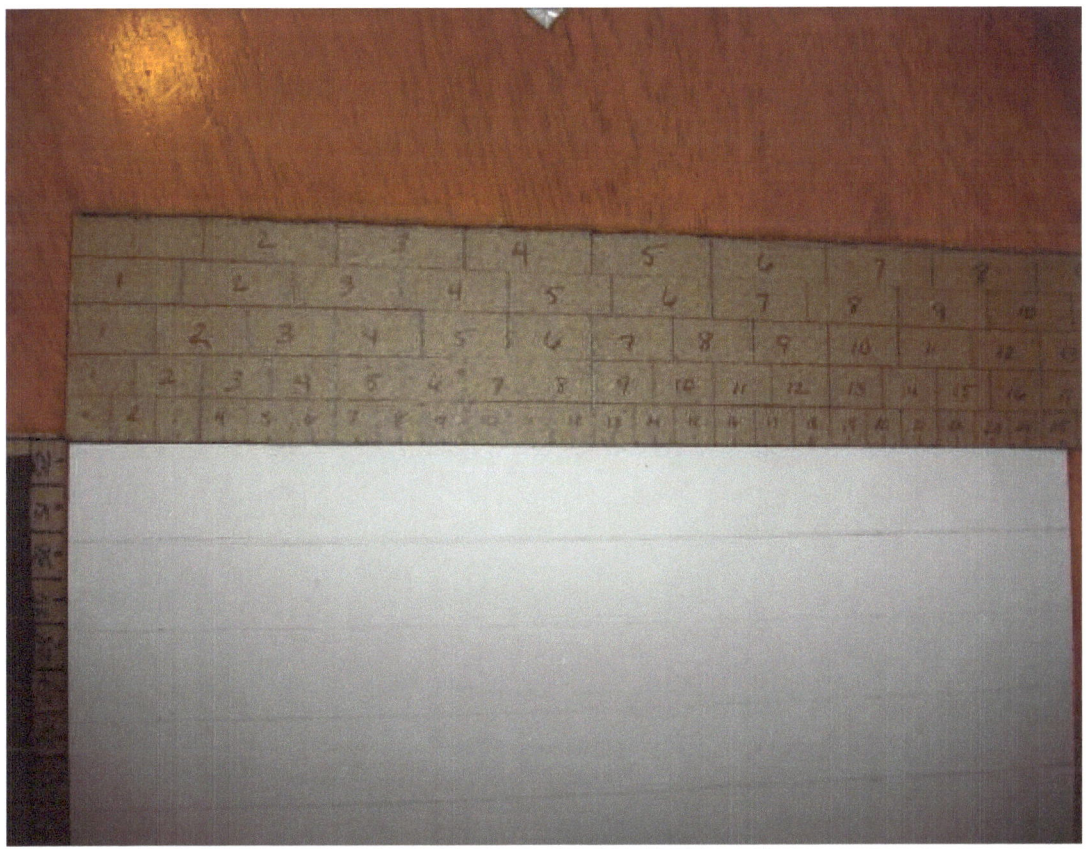

Take one piece of printer paper to fold around your picture holder.

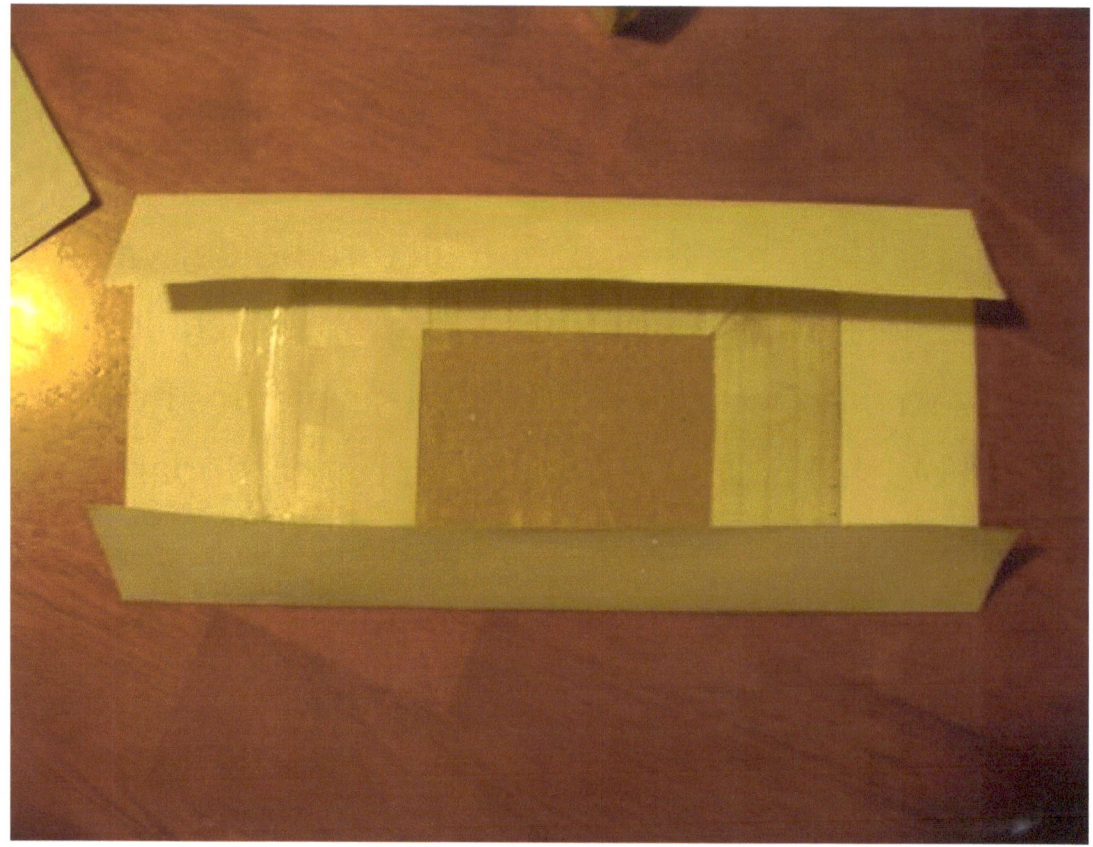

We will attempt to expose the covered part that which does the folded paper now hides. Remove the picture holder from the folded printer paper.

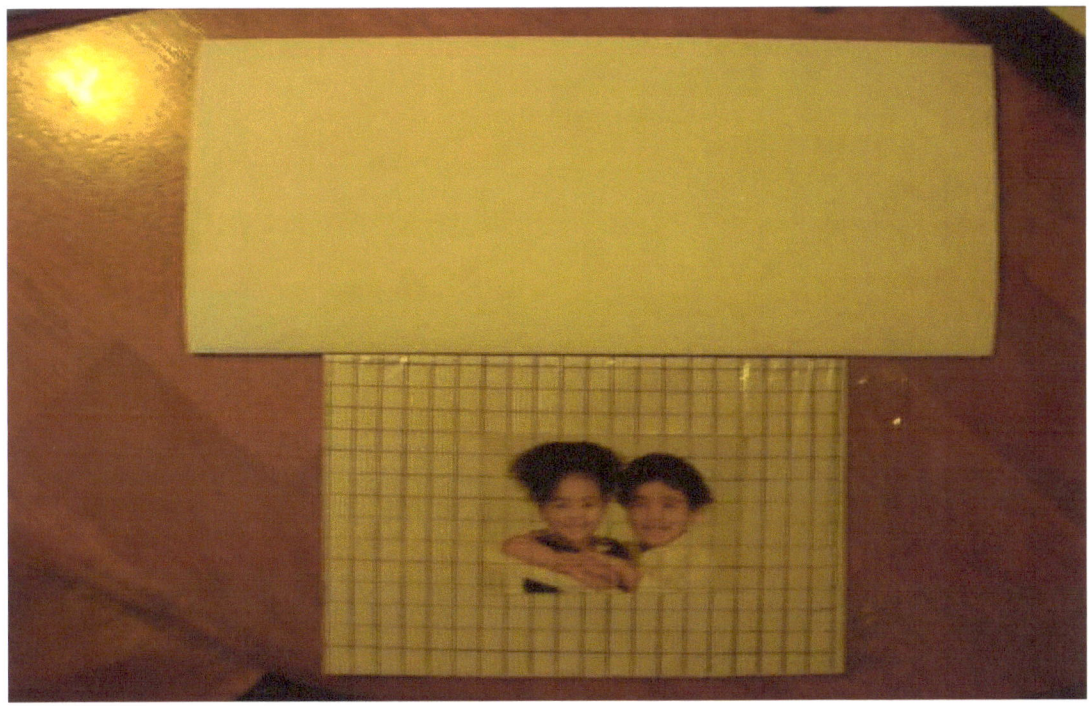

Place the picture holder on top of the folded printer paper. Mark each edge of your holder on your folded printer paper.

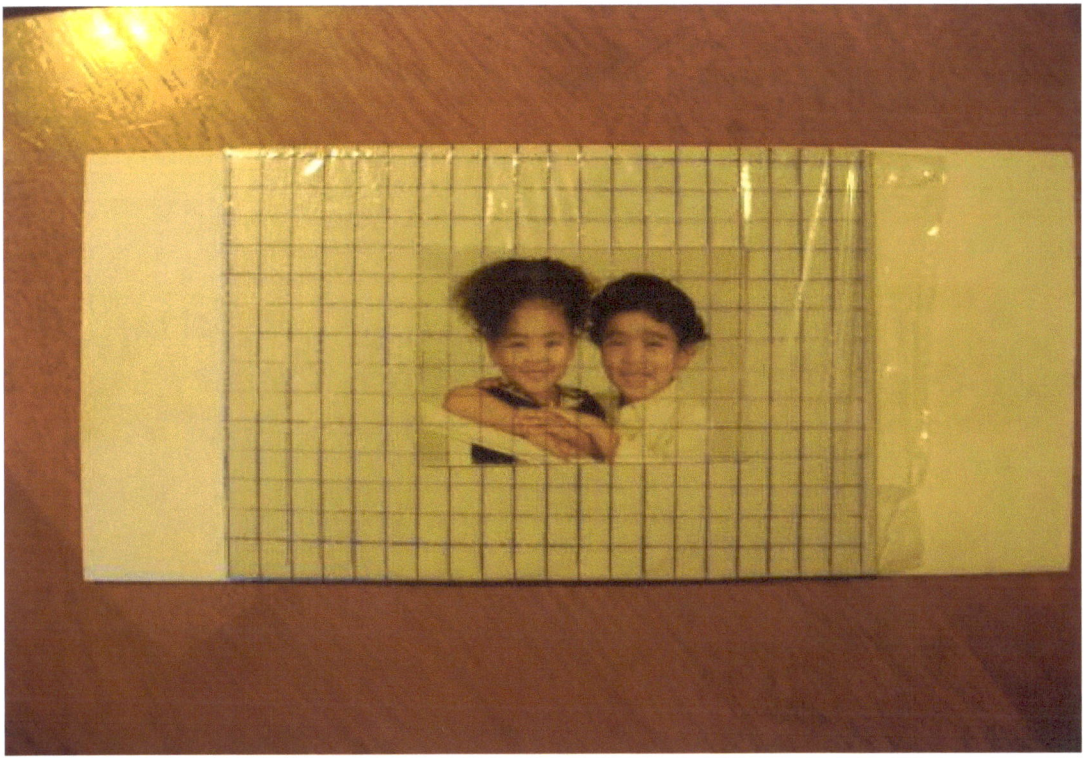

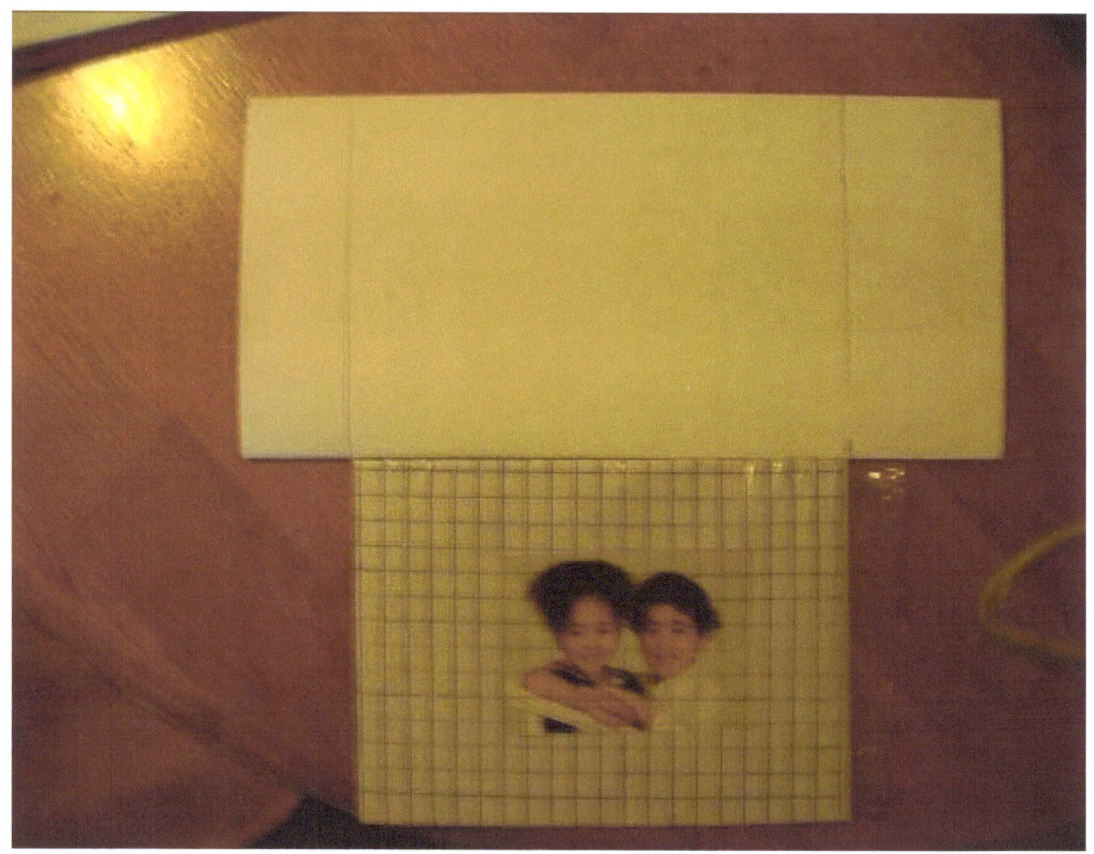

Remove your picture holder from the folded paper Now mark the top and bottom of your folded printer paper. Do the same method for the left and right side of your folded paper.

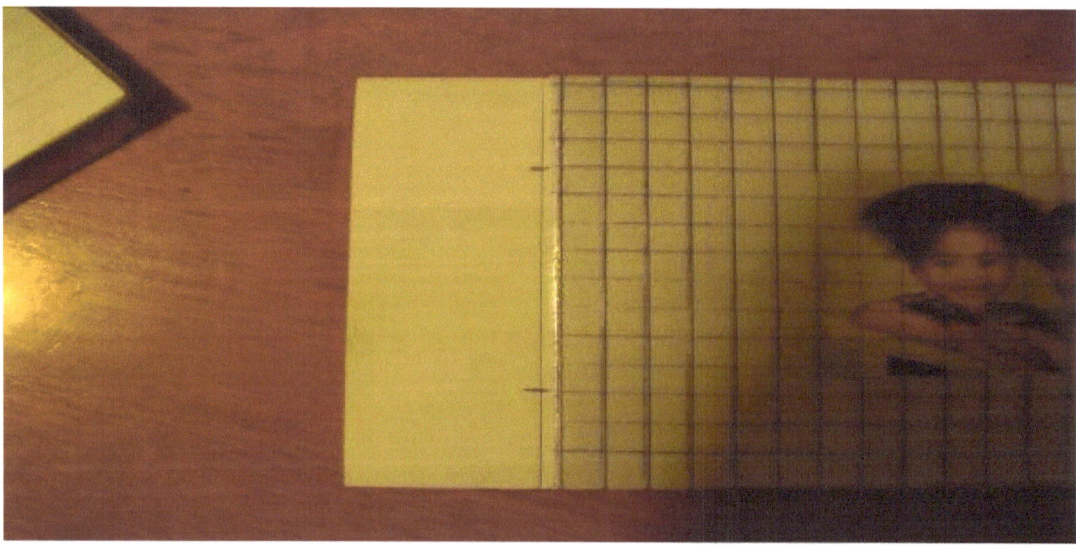

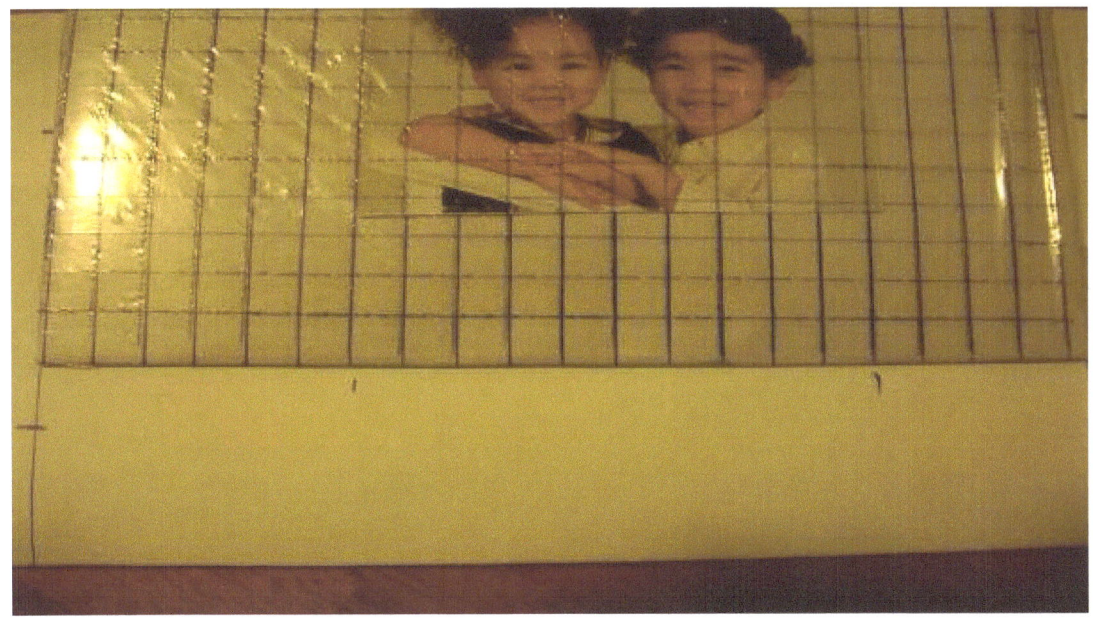

Now mark the top and bottom of your folded paper, remember we are only removing the part of paper that covers your picture.

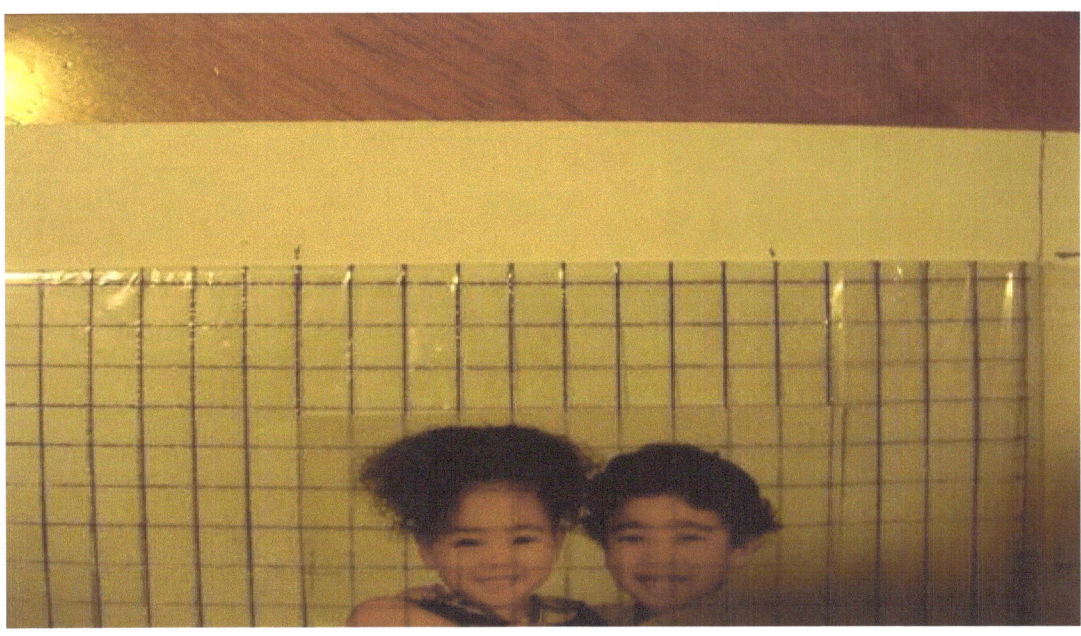

Using your cardboard ruler or regular ruler draw lines connecting the marks made both vertical and horizontal. The X marks the area to be removed exposing your portrait. Remove the printer paper cutting out the part that covers your chosen picture to that spot that is marked X

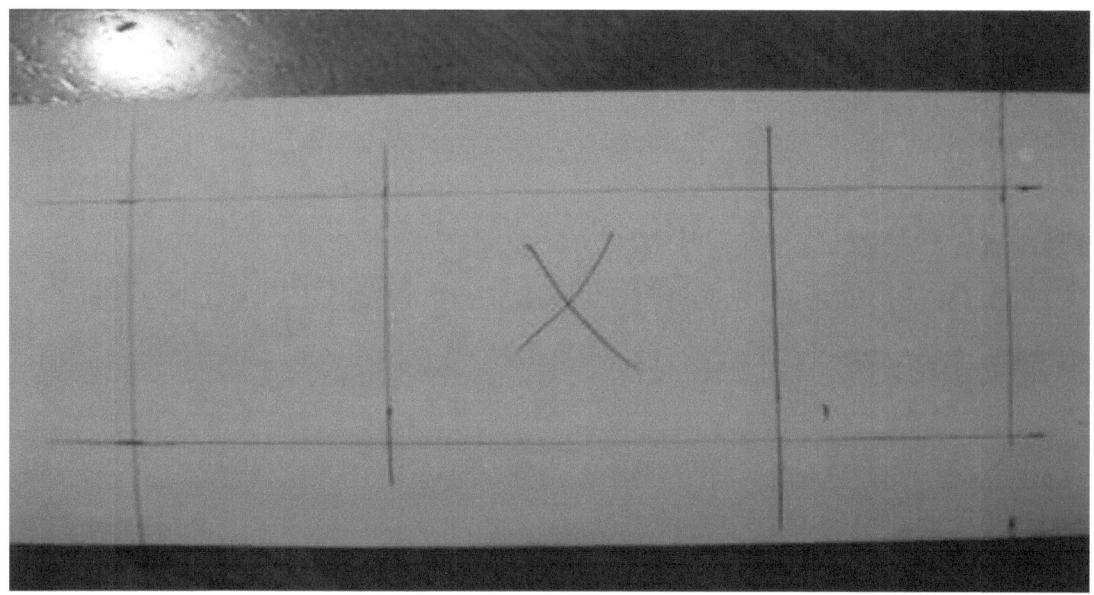

Place the printer paper cover back around your picture holder. We will now begin to count each row both vertical and horizontal.

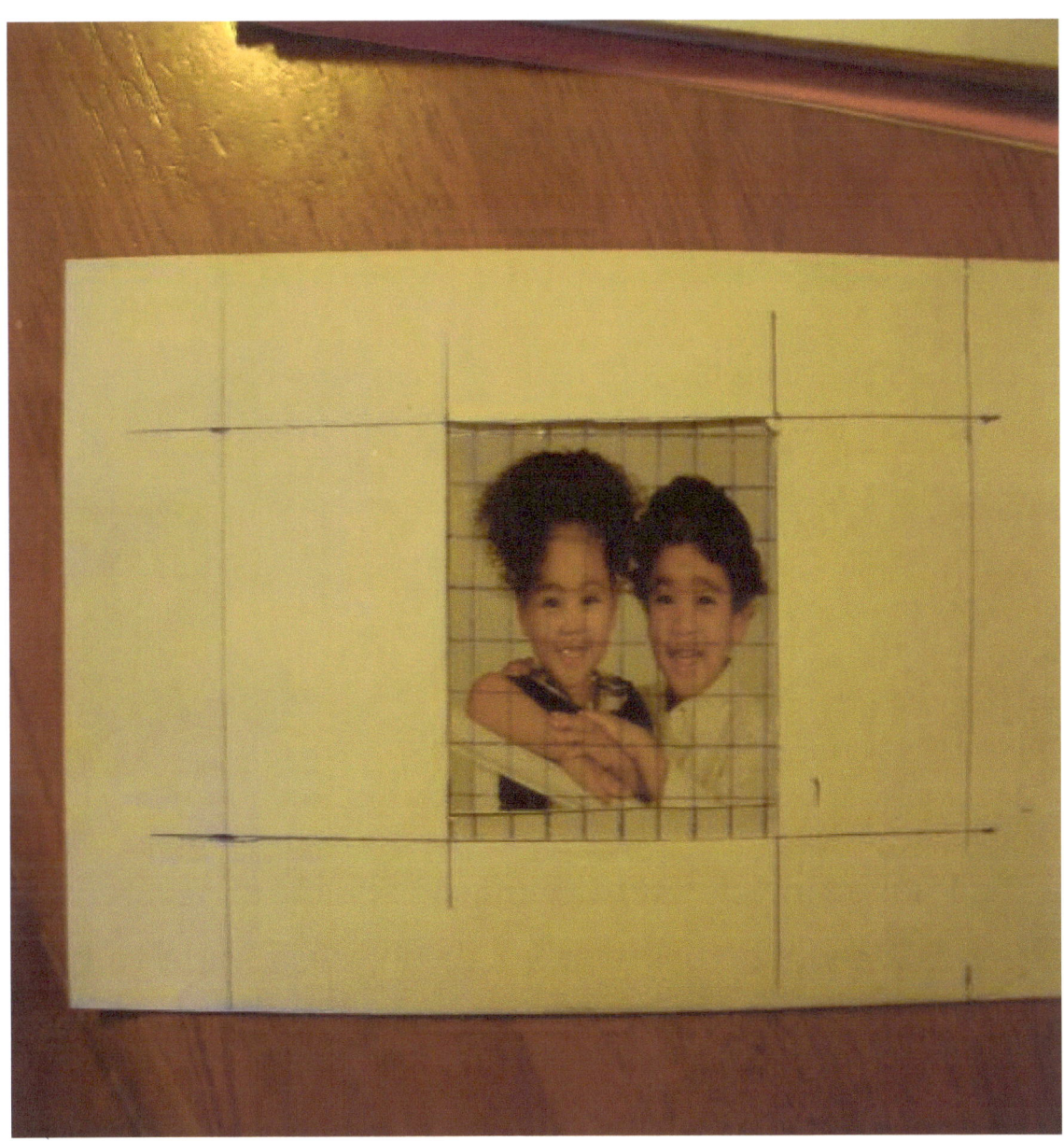

Next we begin to label each row of blocks both vertical and horizontal.

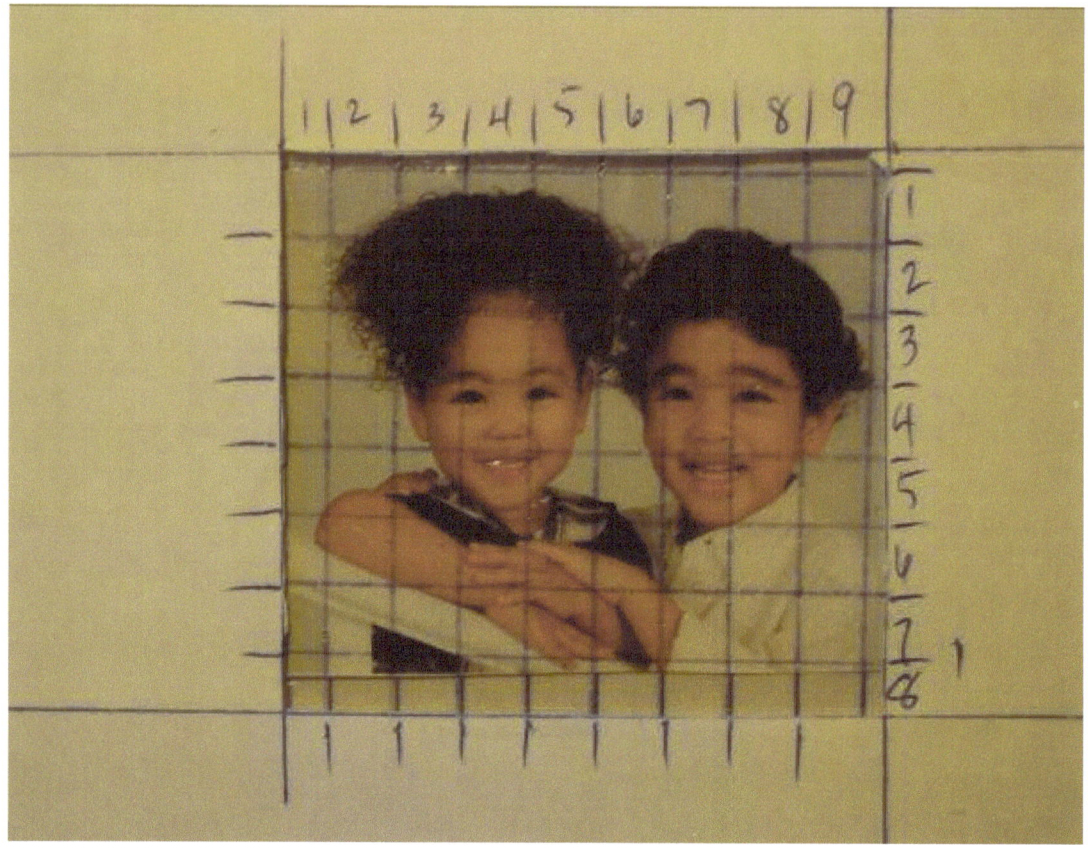

As I have already mentioned my selected picture is 9 by 7. We will be using row 3 of our cardboard ruler to make a grid exactly like the one you see in the above display.

Using row 3, only mark a row of very light marks on your paper you chose to reproduce your chosen portrait.

Make sure you mark the bottom in the same fashion as you marked the top from left to right taking care that you are using row 3 and only row 3. This exercise will produce an evenly row of vertical lines to match that of your picture holder.

Remember to lightly draw your lines; we will later erase these lines. Using the same row on your cardboard ruler row 3, align your ruler horizontally just as you did vertically

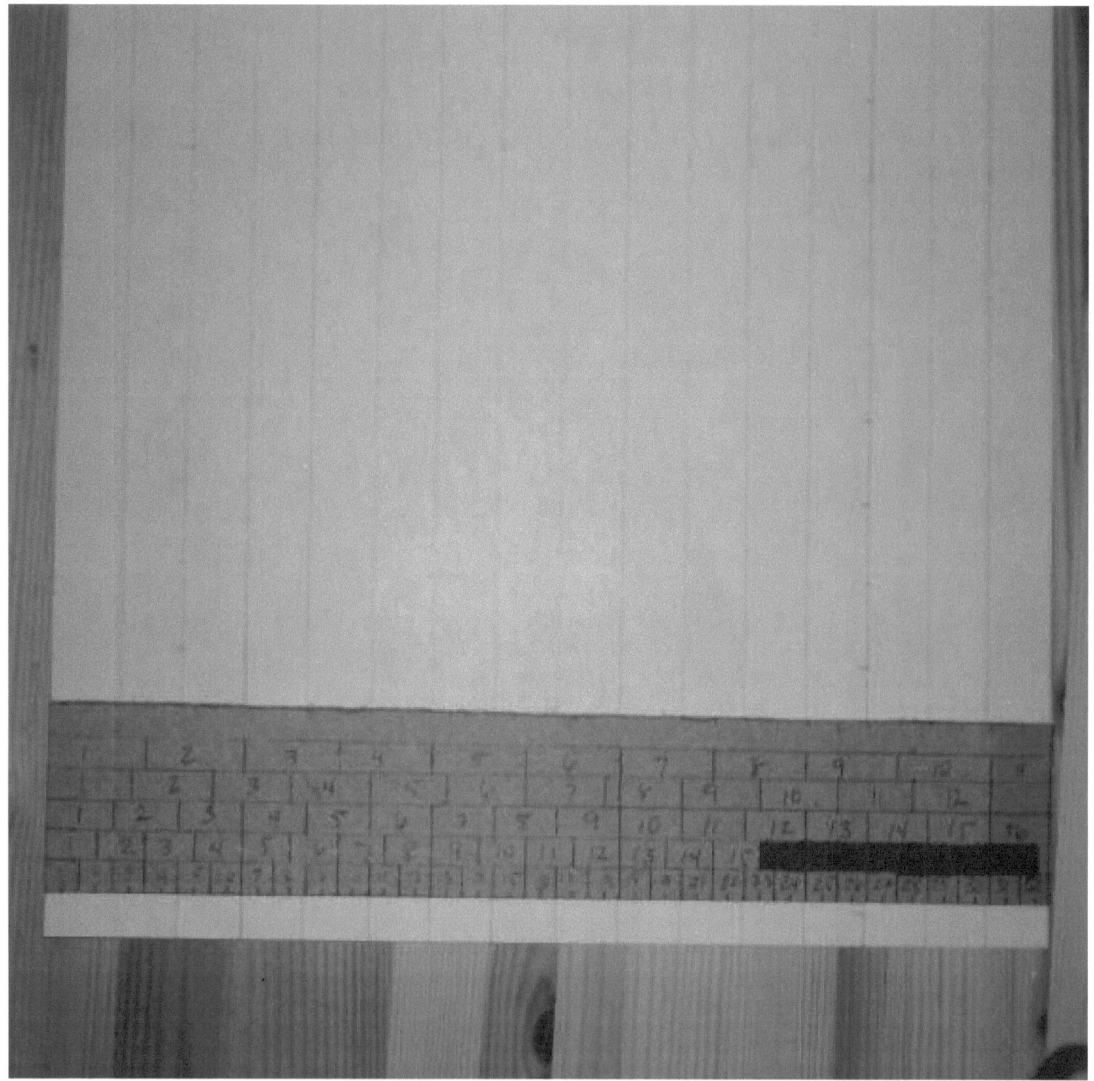

After making your marks in the same fashion you did vertically we are now ready to connect our marks horizontally using your regular school ruler.

After completing the lines horizontally and vertically your paper should look exactly like the picture holder holding your proposed picture to draw.

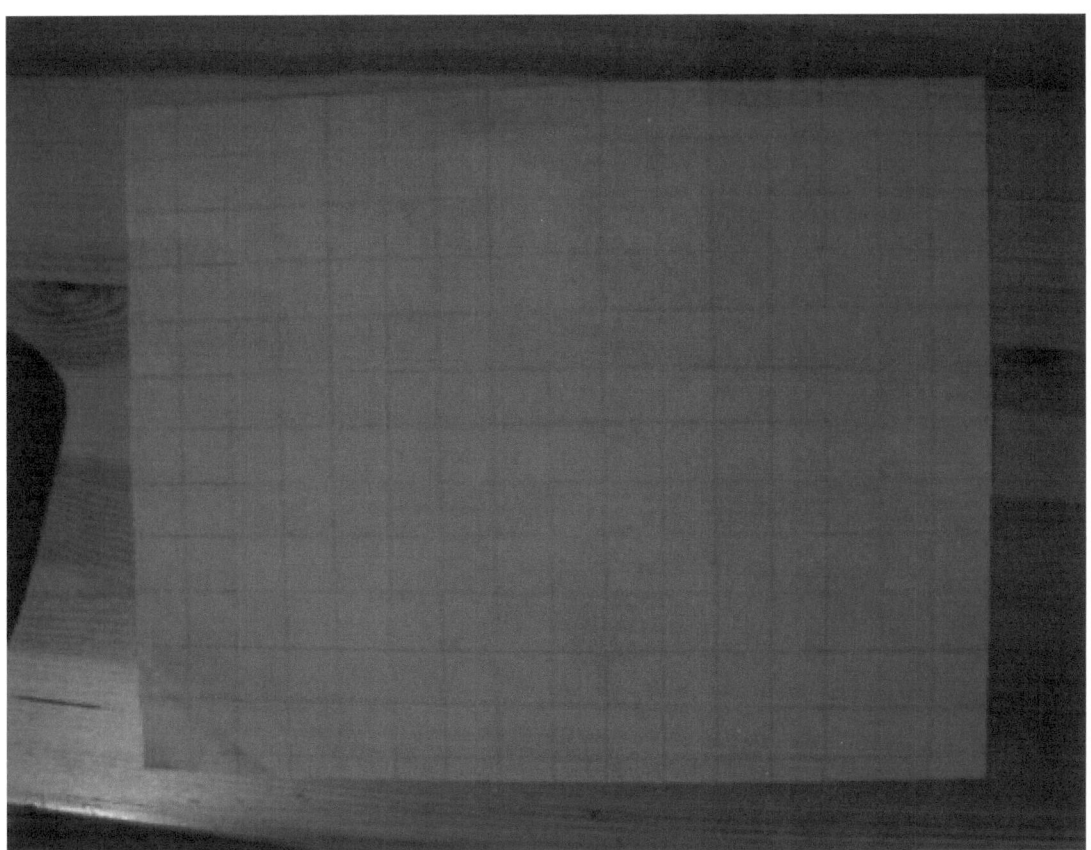

Our next step will be to center your portrait on your chosen printer paper. My particular paper is 9 by 8.

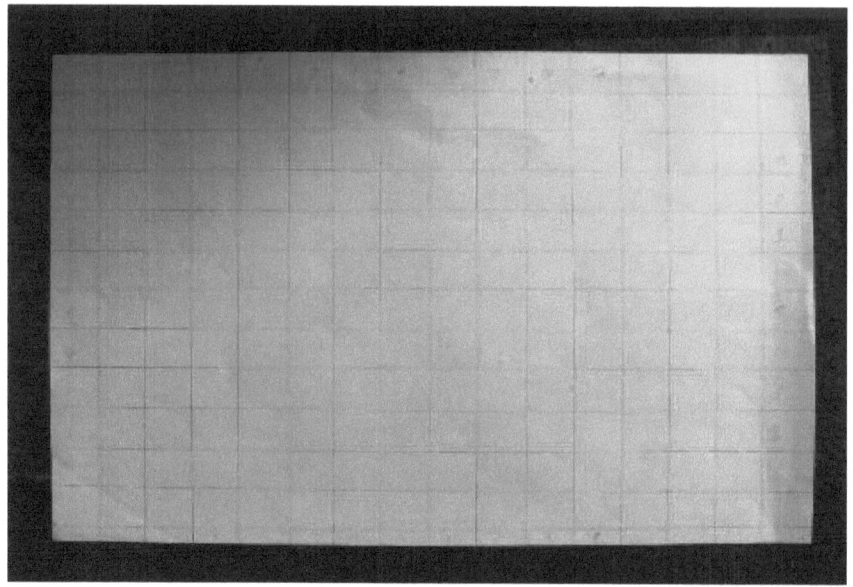

We begin by counting all blocks in the top most row of your chosen project paper. My paper is 16 blocks by subtracting 9 from 16 that leaves 7 blocks to be divided, either 3 empty blocks, then begin to number your blocks 1 to 9 leaving 4 empty blocks on the right or vice verse.

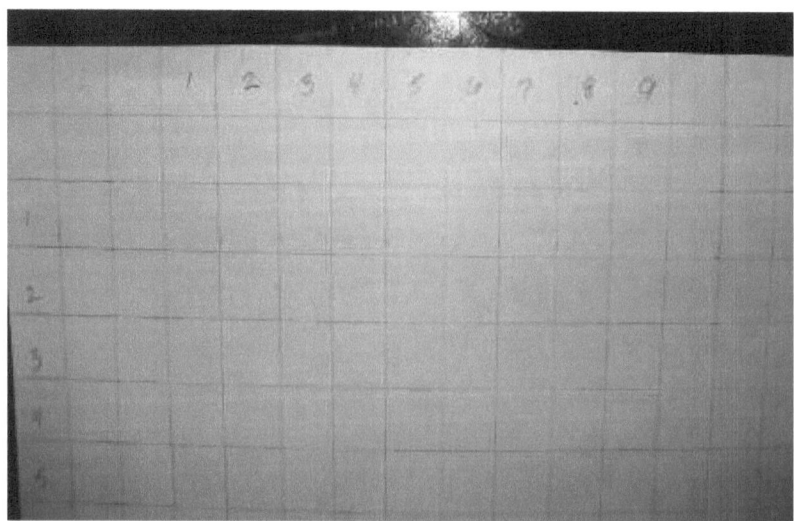

Now count the row of blocks going down, which is 12 on my paper. Subtracting 8 from 12 leaves 4 blocks to be divided with 2 empty first row blocks then number your blocks 1 to 8 leaving to empty blocks at the bottom.

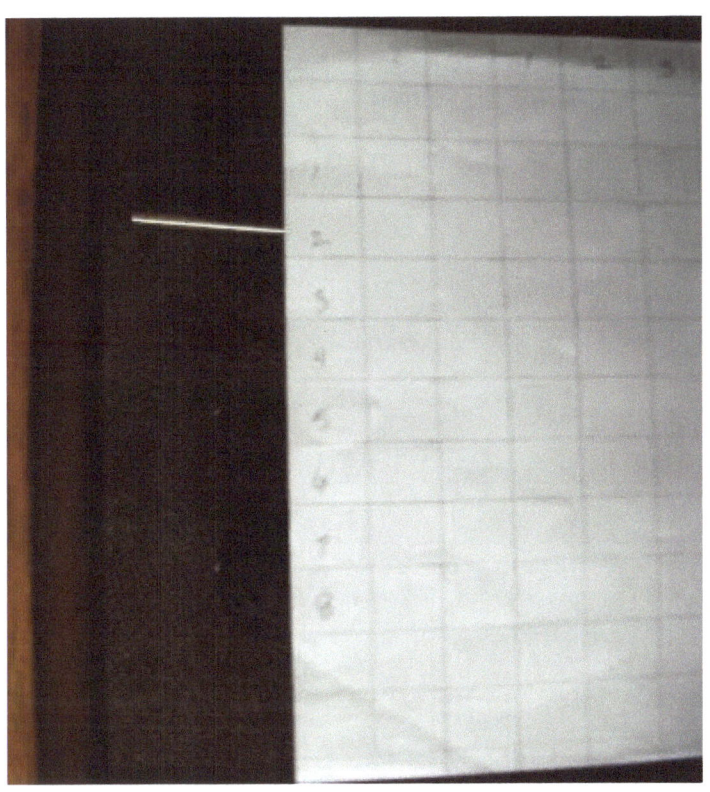

Now it time to draw, we begin by cross referencing from your picture holder to your chosen paper. We begin by outlining the entire picture. Drawing that which is only shown in your numbered blocks by cross referencing using your top row and your right row of numbers. Then proceed to draw the inside your picture such as the eyes, nose, and lips. Remember to use your numbers and blocks to know exactly where your eyes, nose, and lips should be.

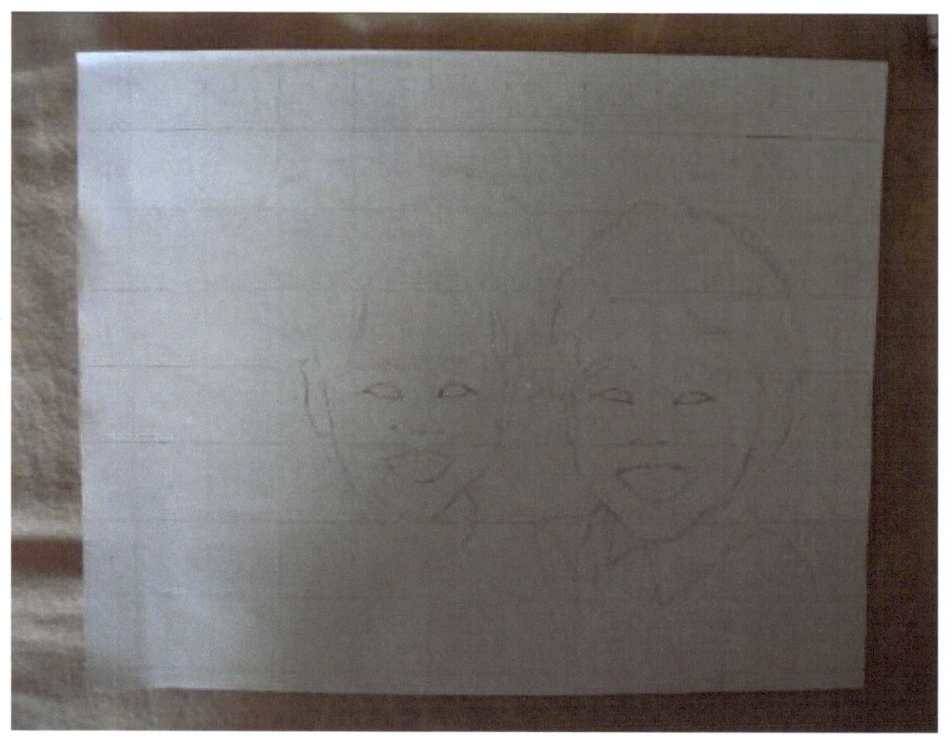

Remember these lines should be lightly drawn, so
that you may be able to change any lines that may
need changing as well as deleted. Once you have
completely drawn a silhouette of your picture.
We no longer need the picture holder we now have
an unmistakable likeness of the particular picture you
chosen. Remove the picture from the picture holder.
We will now fine tune our picture before we proceed
any further. How we do this is by closely examining
all facets of your portrait to see what does not suite
your eyes, for an example: I pay very close attention
to the eyes making sure they are close to the likeness
of the picture as possible there may need to be some
adjustment of your silhouette until you are satisfied
that you have a unmistakable likeness.

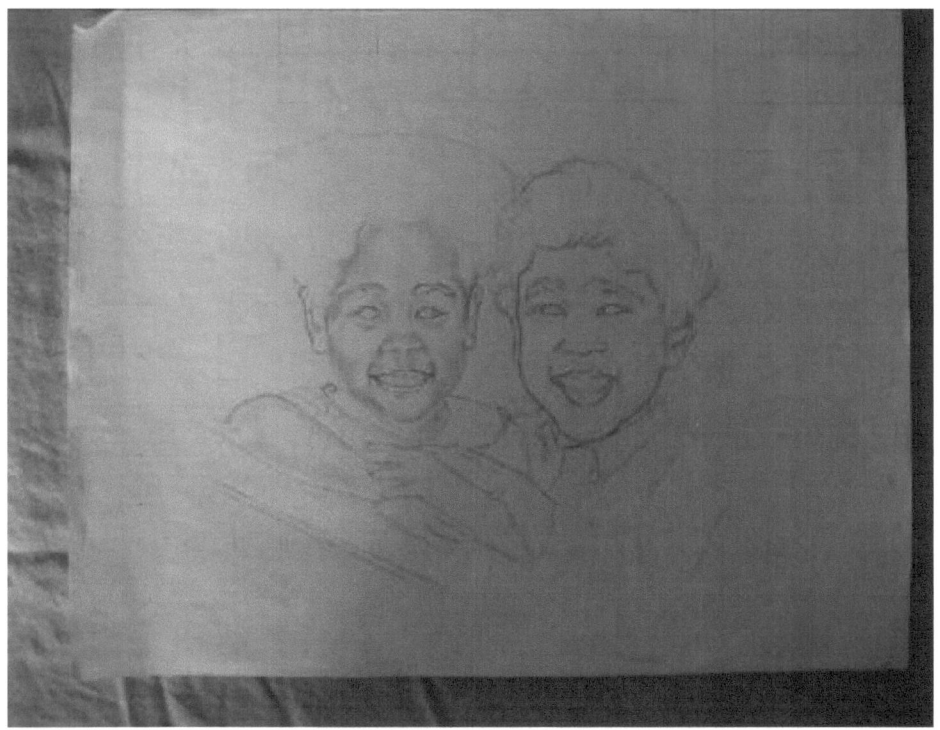

Remember to draw softly and lightly and to fine tune your picture in every way. Pay close attention to the inside details of your portrait like the nose, eyes, lips, shape and the appearance of your picture.

Chapter 6 – constructing your personal shaders

Before we go any further we now have to create shaders, there are two ways, to purchase them or make your own. I prefer to make my own. I use newspaper preferably no colorful portions of the paper.

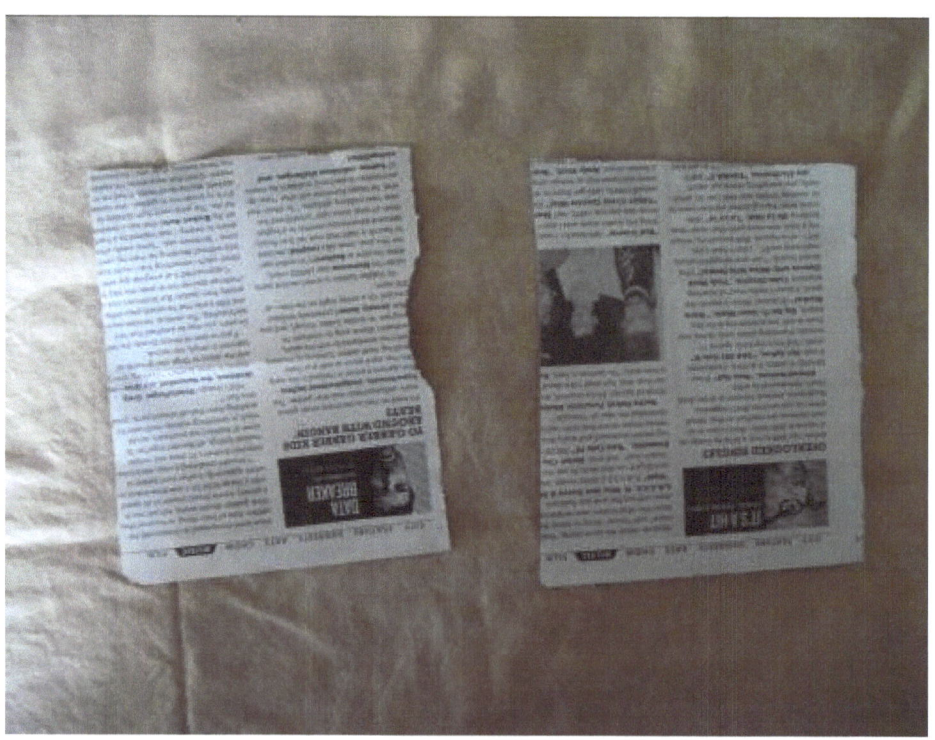

We will be creating two types of shaders, one for small tight area this particular shader needs to have a sharp tip, I use this one to shade around the eyes nose and lips, and one for larger areas such as the cheeks forehead and jaw or for pictures with parts of the body included.

Fold your chosen piece of paper in half.

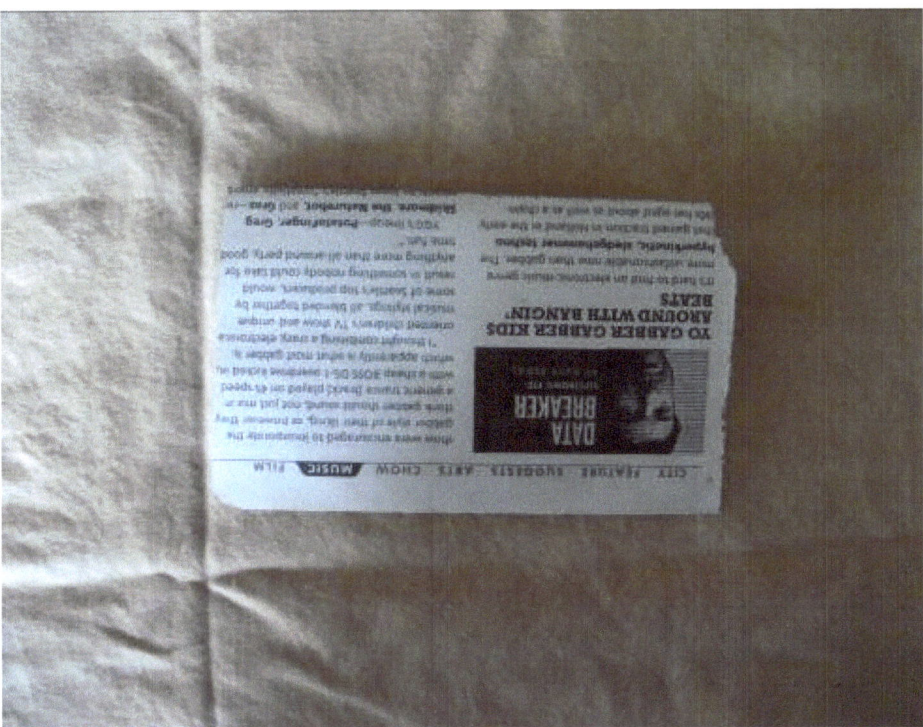

Again fold your paper in half.

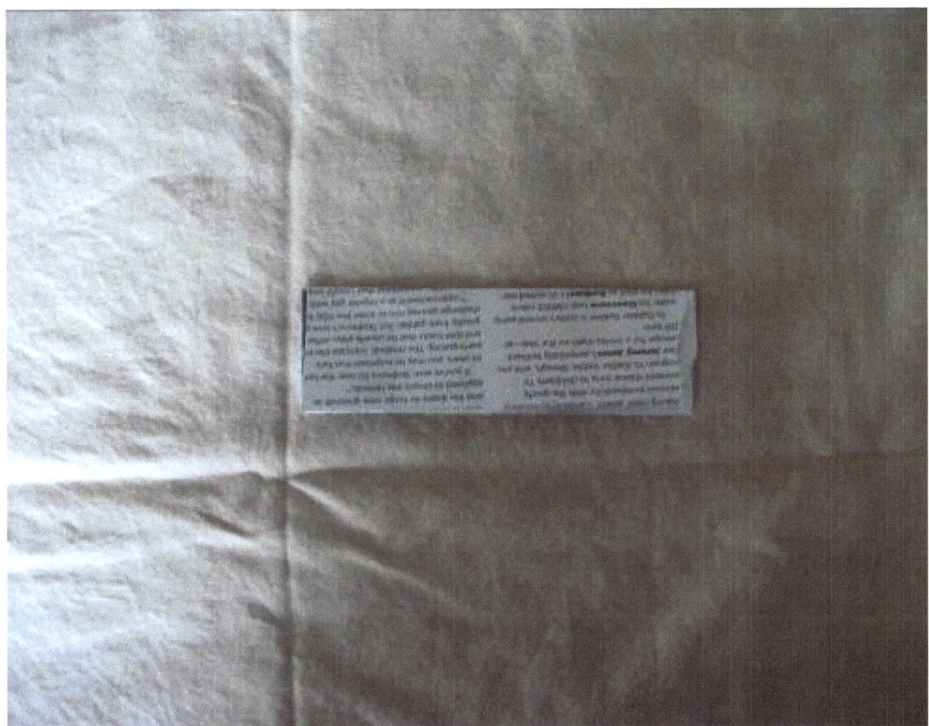

Once more fold your paper in half.

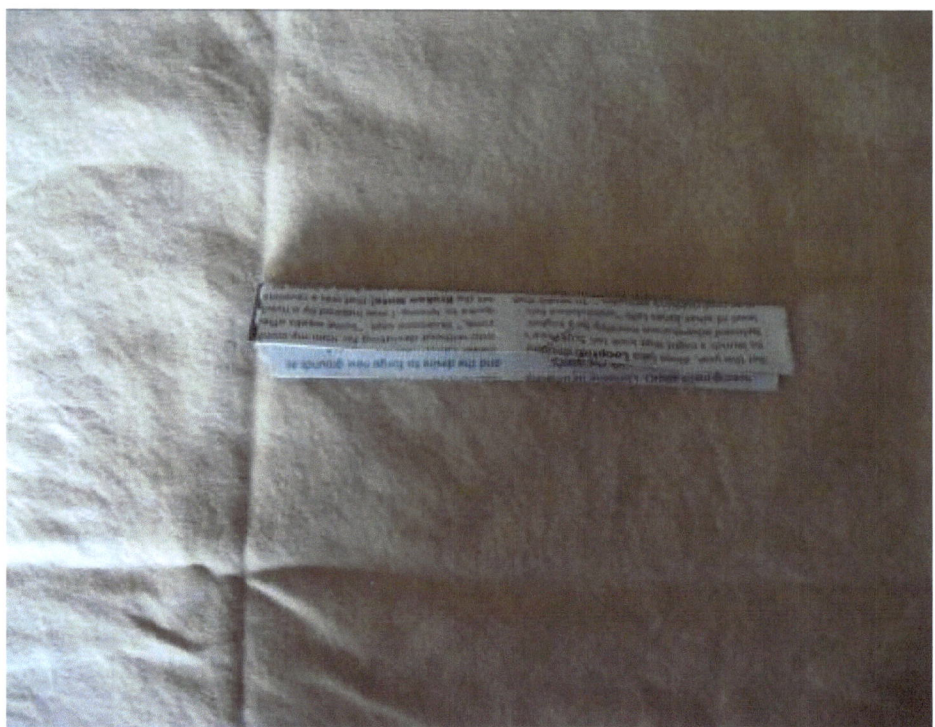

Now fold your paper into an L shape like shown below.

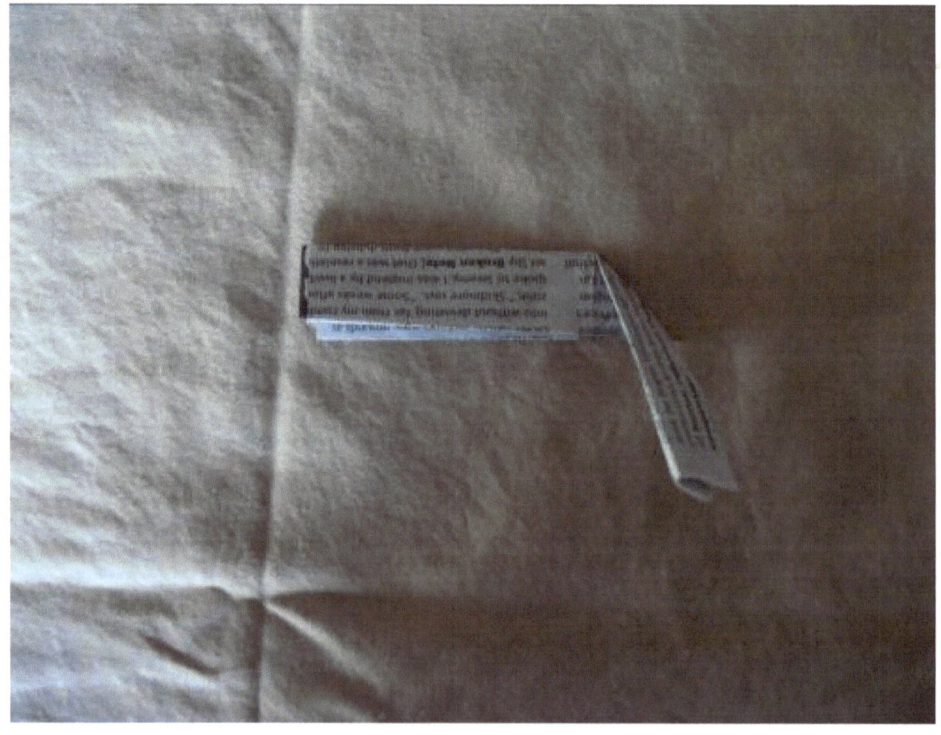

Fold the other side to meet your opposite side you first folded.

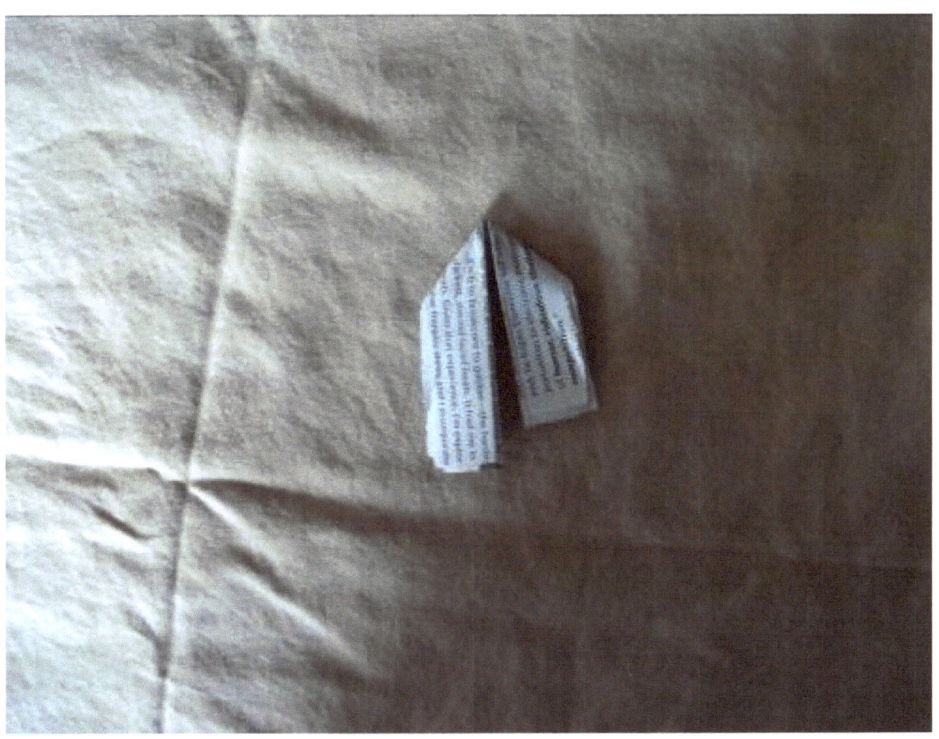

Fold in half each of the now fold sides.

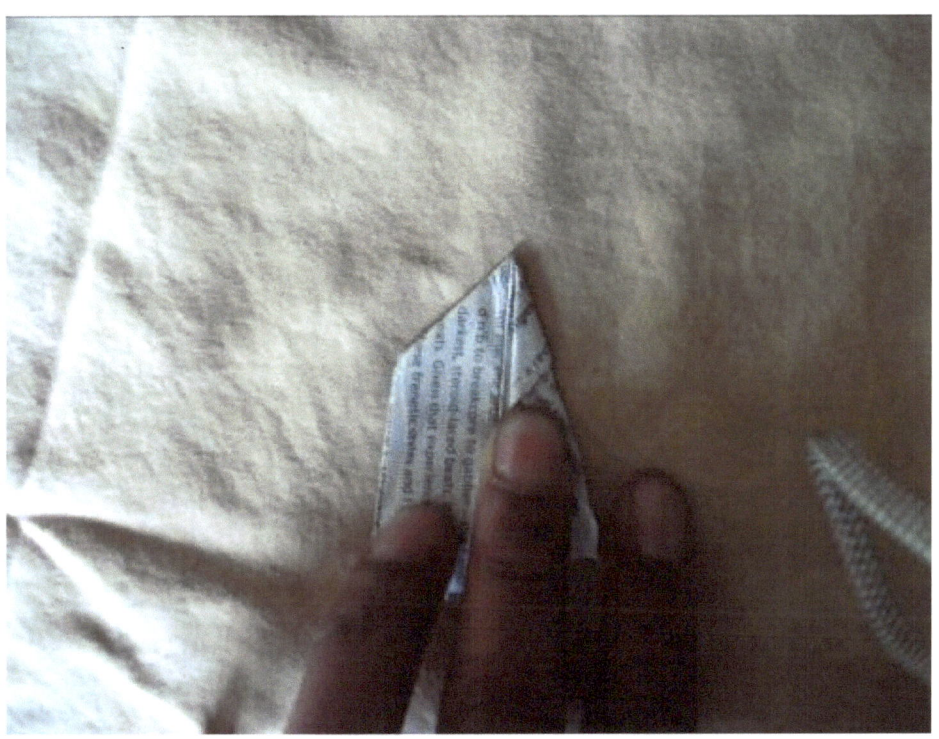

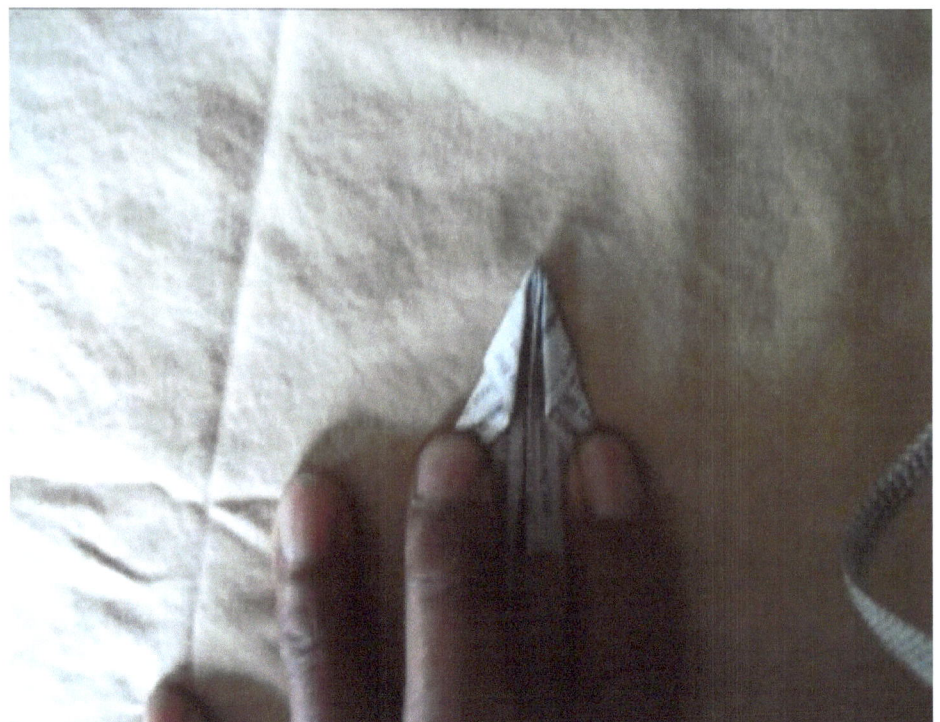

For your last and final fold bring both ends together to create a sharp pencil like shader shown below, remember to tape your shader so it will stay together.

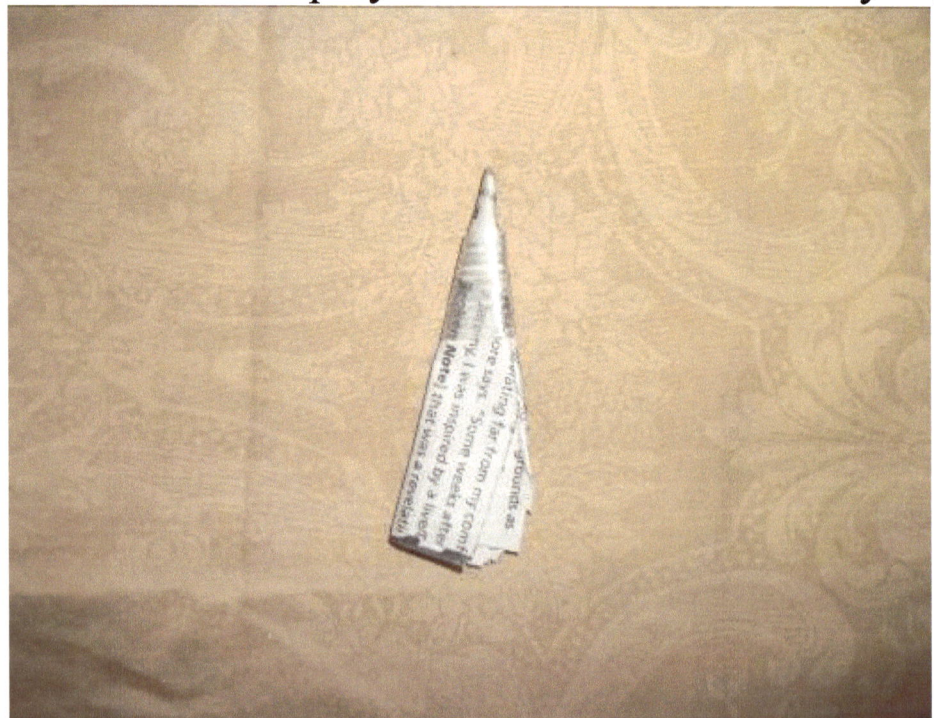

Now we have just completed the making of one shader. Remember to use this one for the finer areas in your picture.

On to the next shader, this one is used for the larger areas that need to be shaded. Take the last piece of paper chosen for your shader. Place one a flat surface take a little water and pour over your paper, starting from the bottom end of your paper fold the lower bottom portion to be rolled into the likeness of a pencil. Once completely rolled, continue to role your shader over and over using a book to apply pressure as to make a tight solid shader.

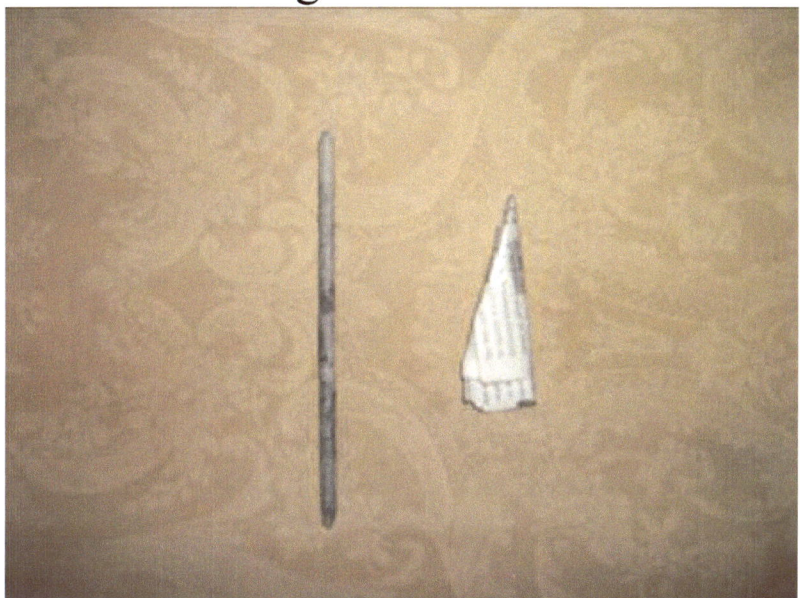

Now we are ready to shade and bring your picture to life. Shading is another issue of course it takes practice, practice and more practice to get your shading to a point where your picture sells itself once you're done. I have also included for your viewing the many pictures in the past I have completed using this method. Each and every drawn picture inserted was done using this method I have just shared with you in my book. I hope this method will help you in your steps to becoming an outstanding artist. Thank you for choosing my book.

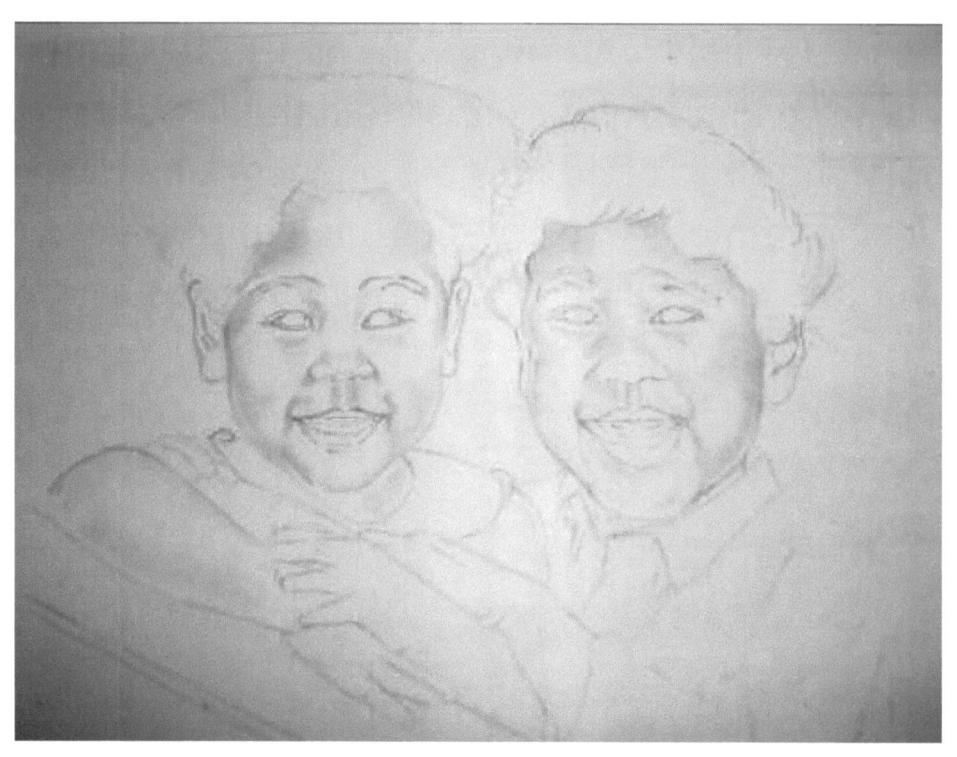

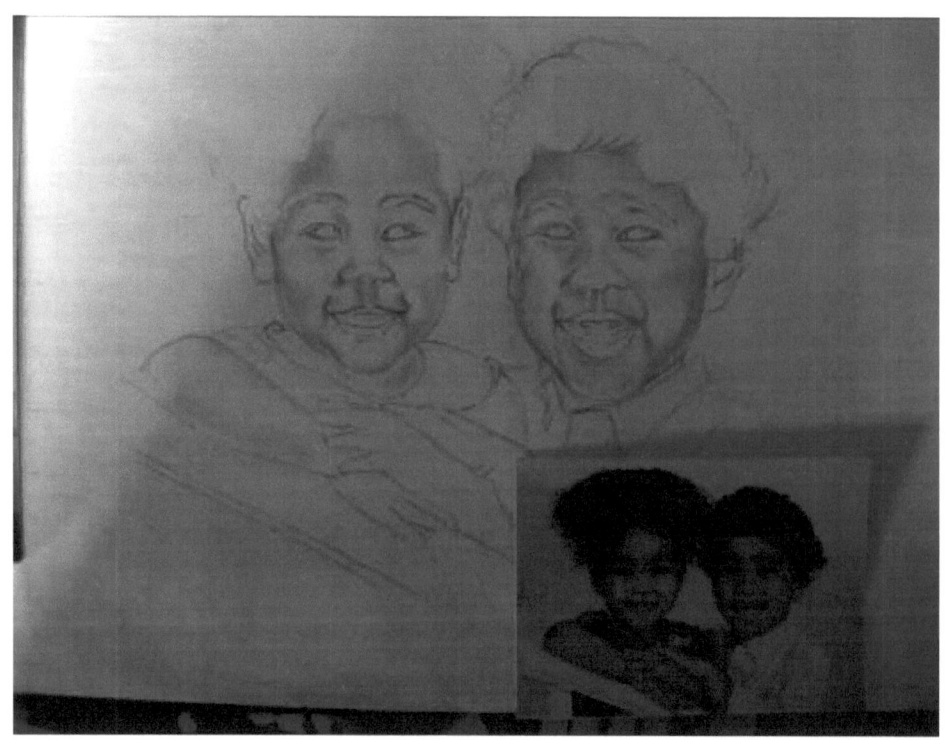

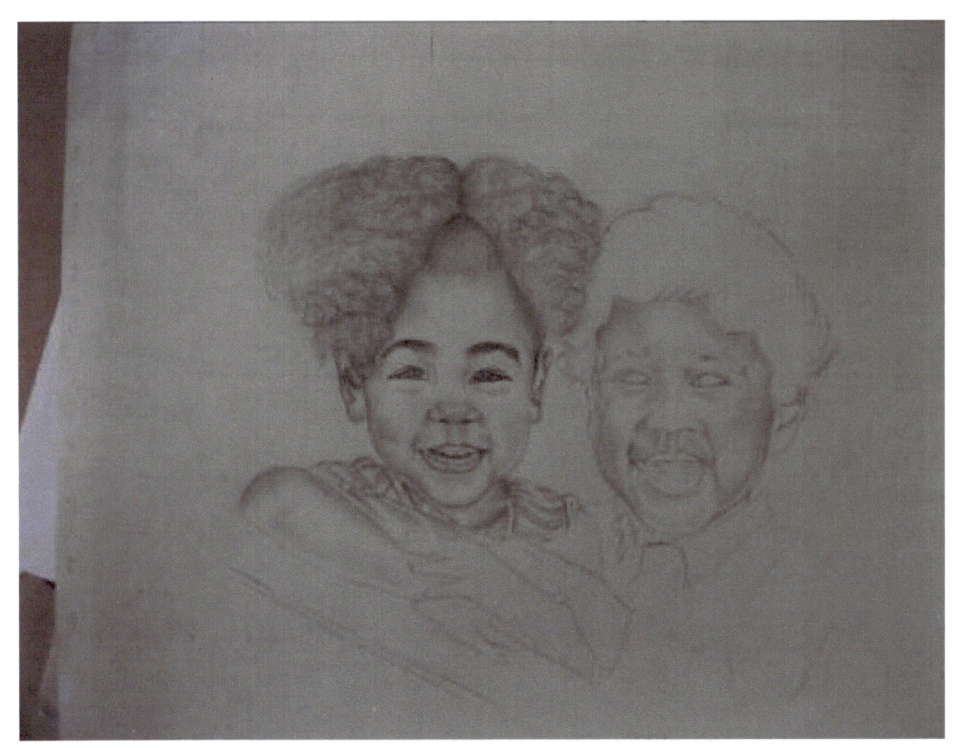

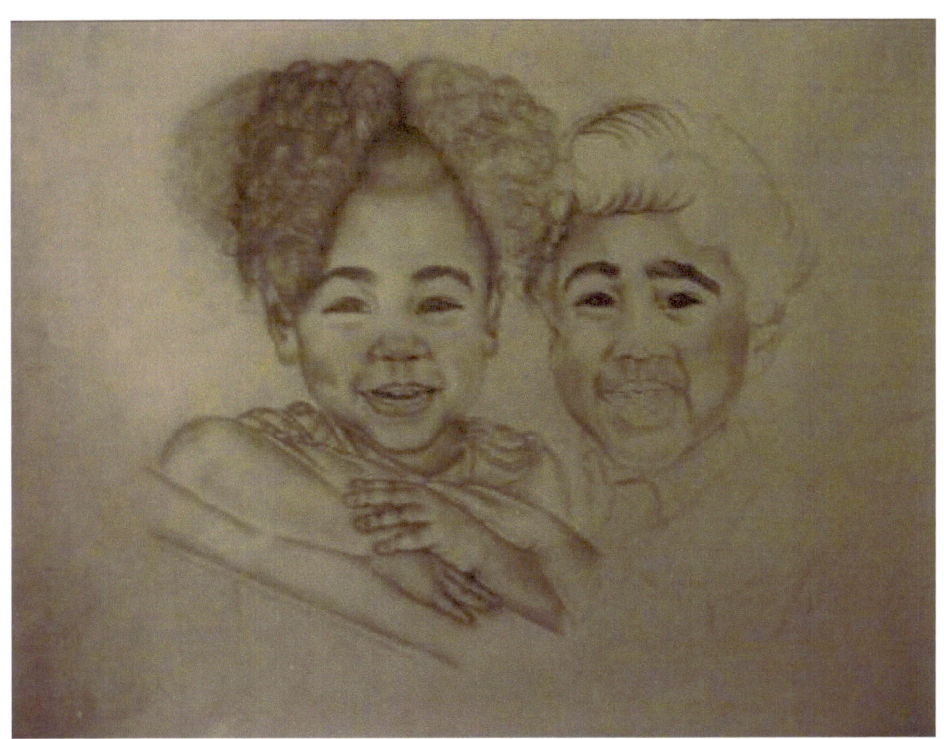

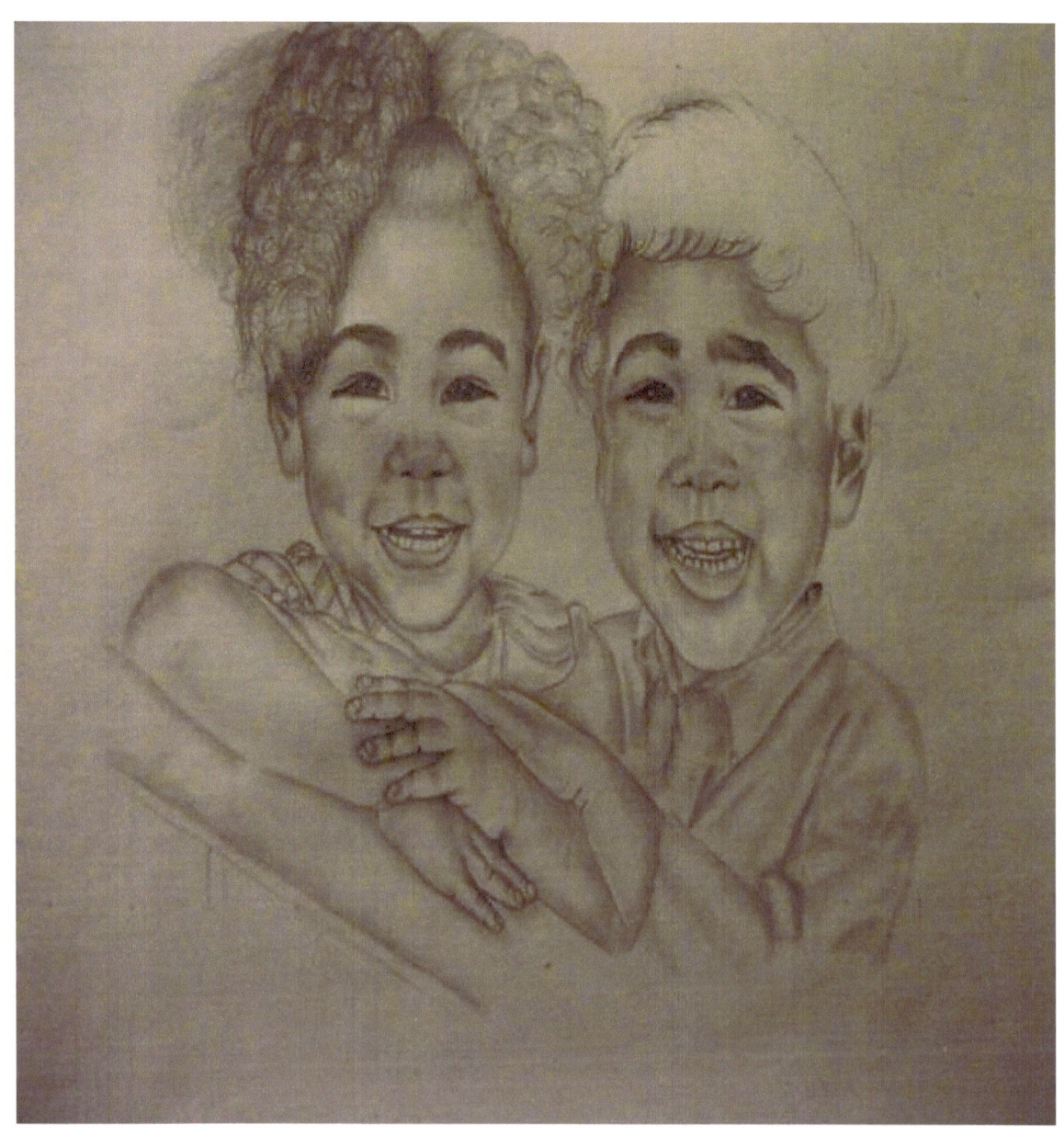

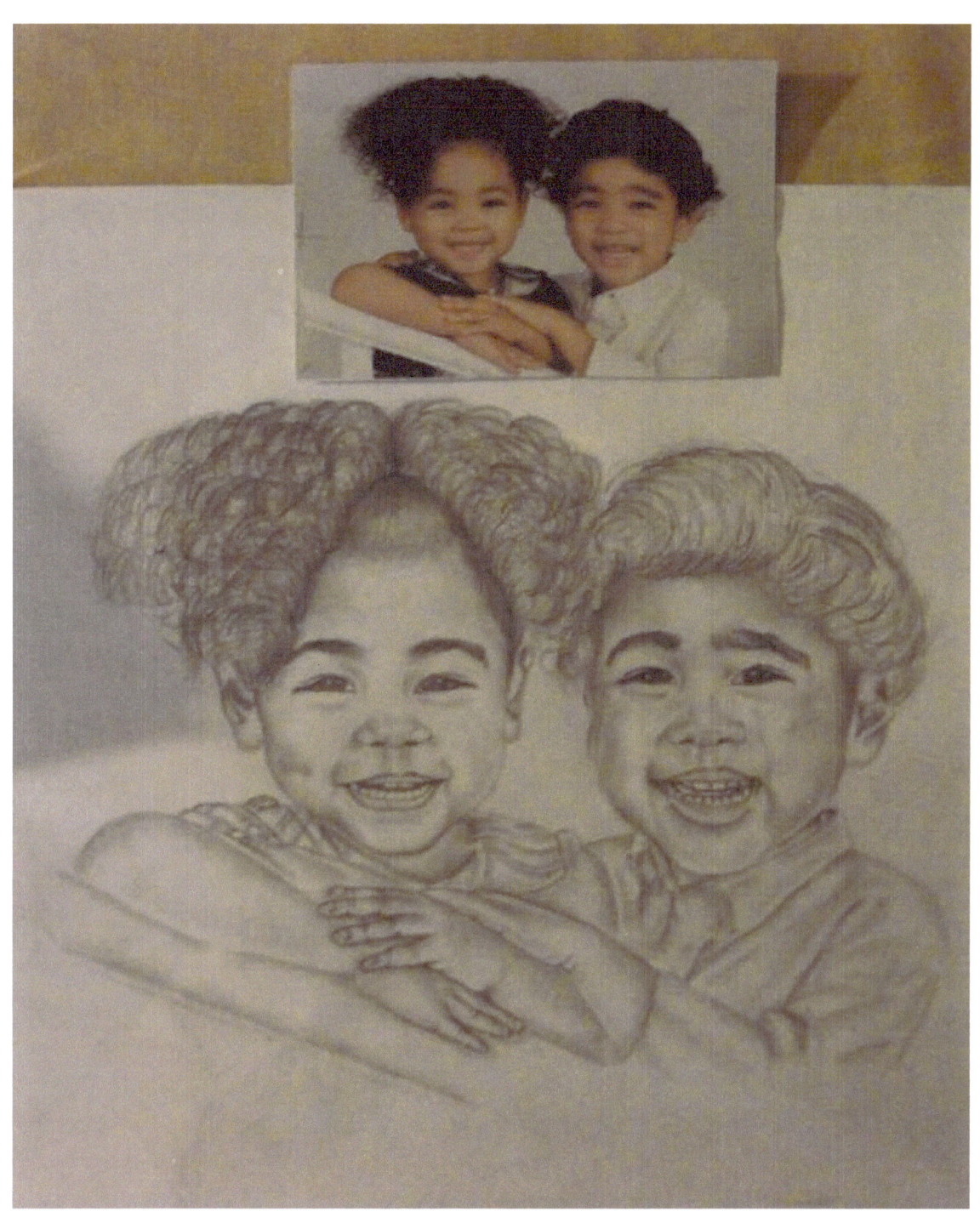

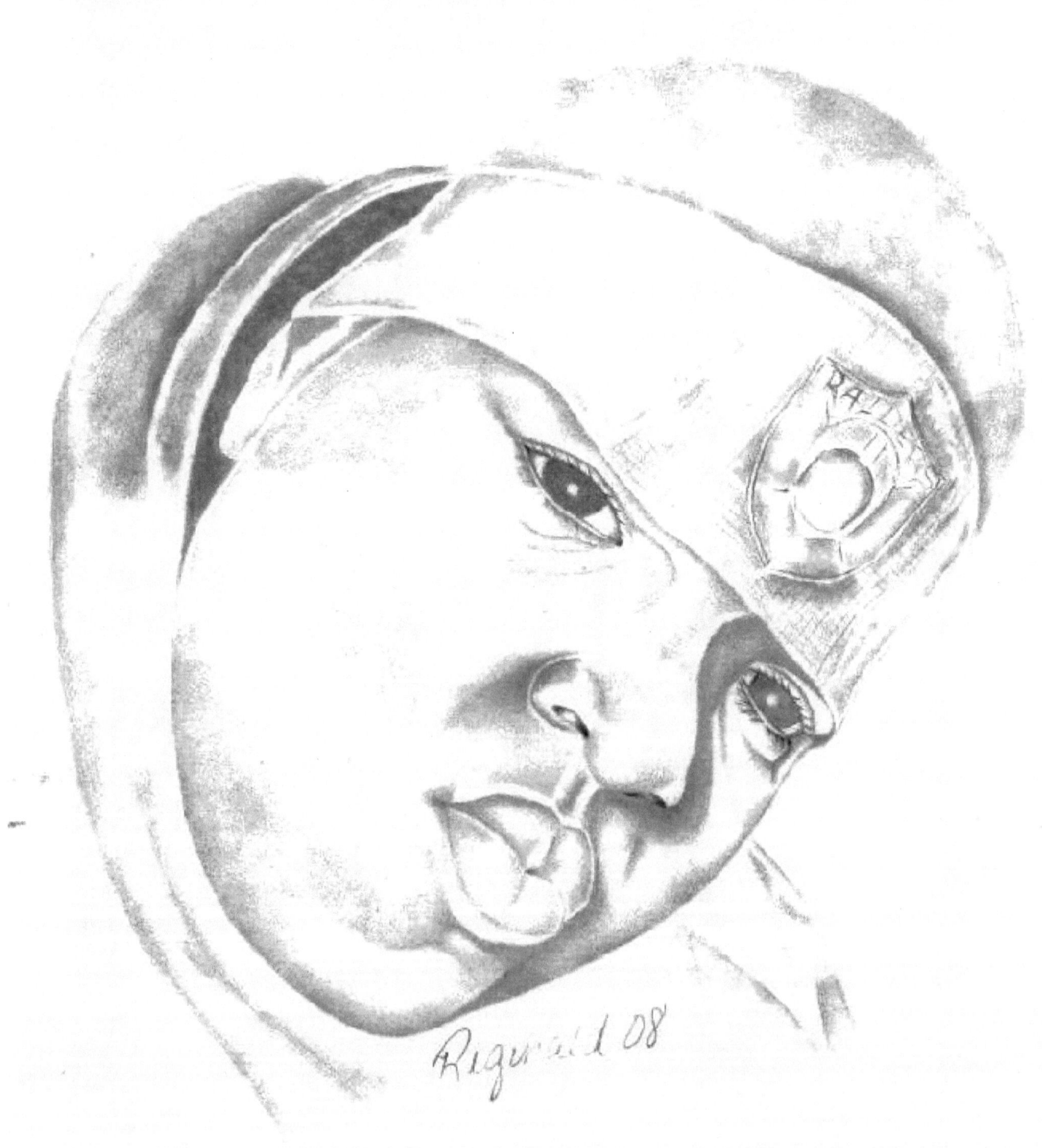

Ricquird 08

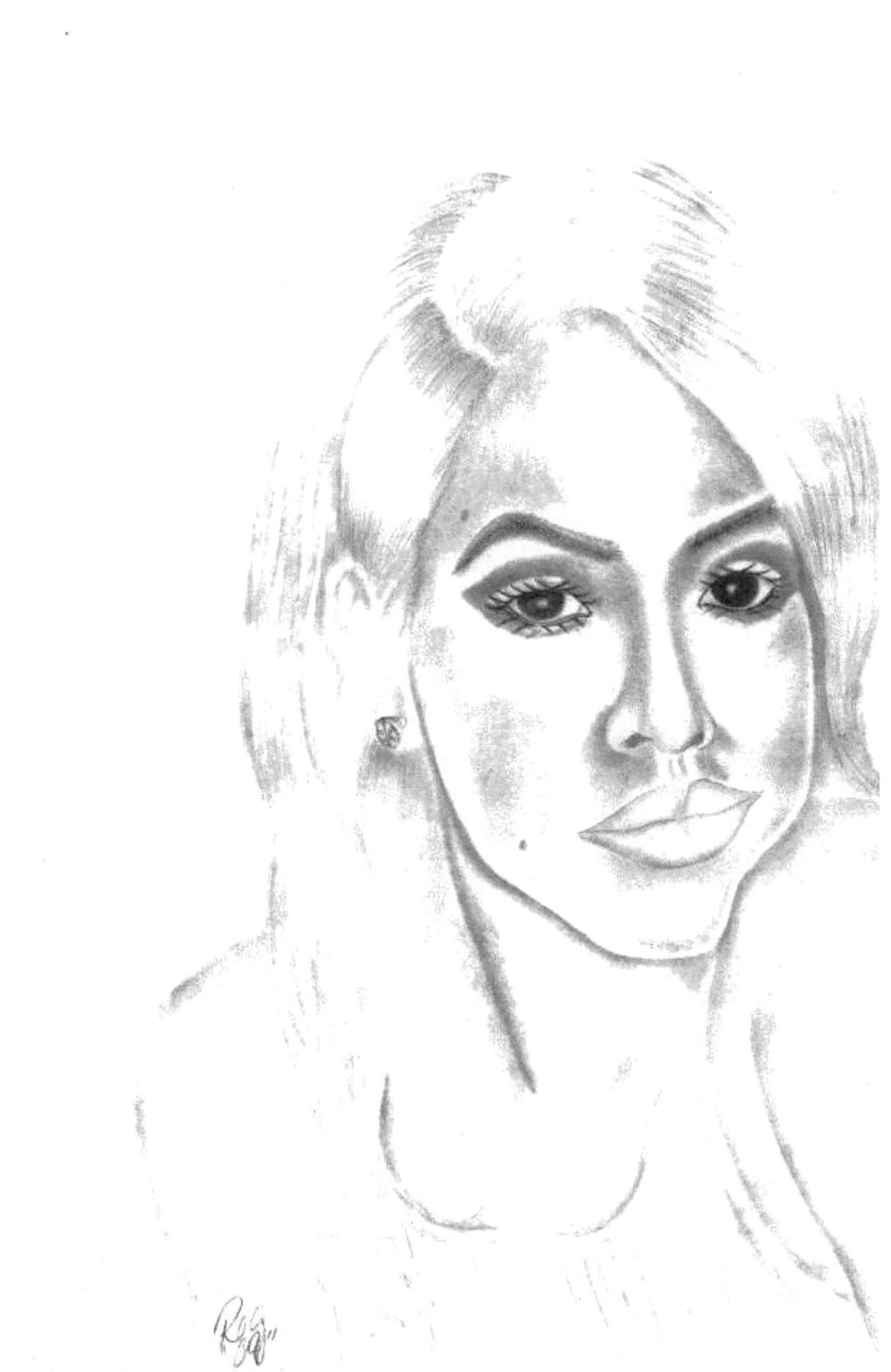

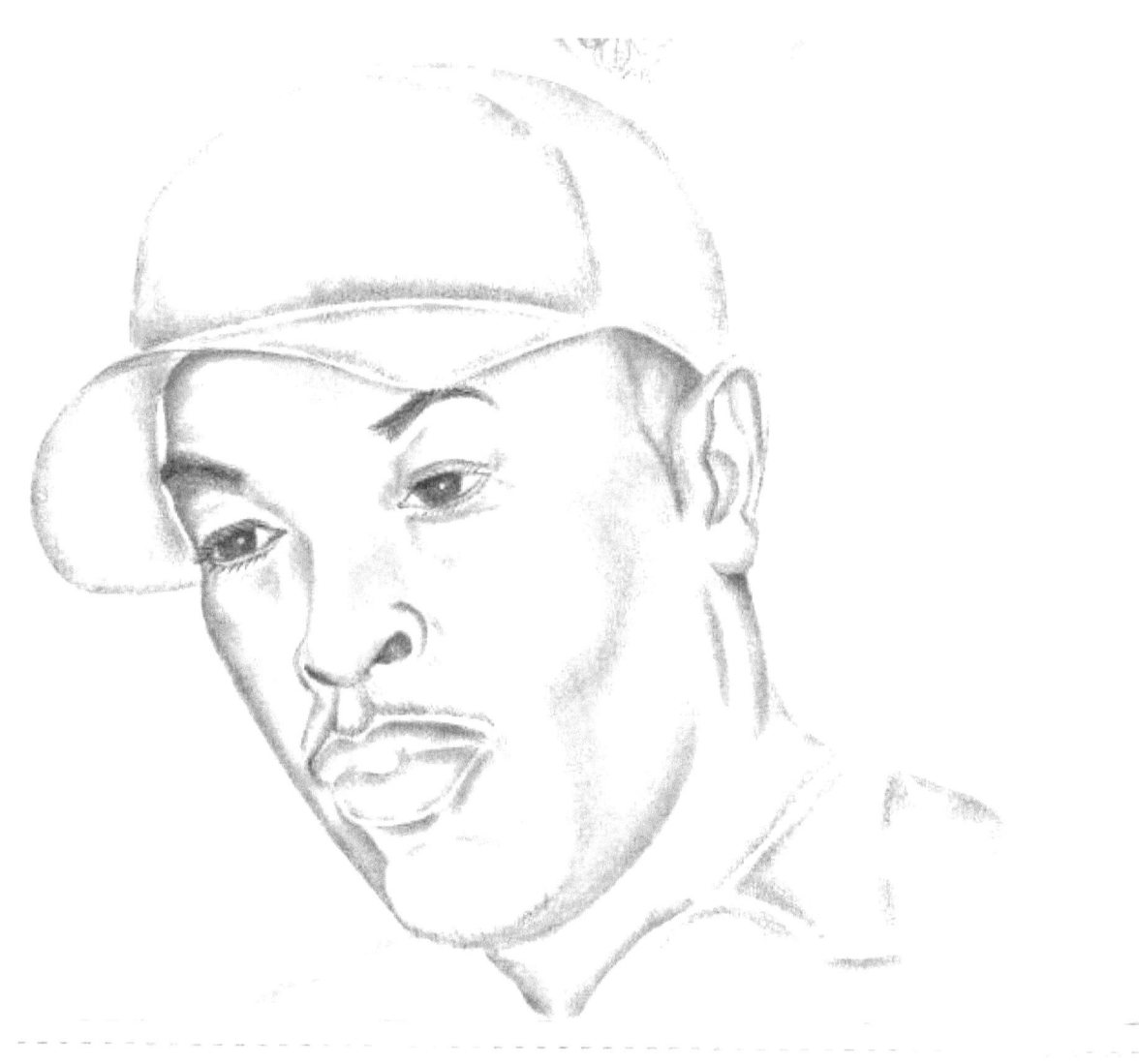

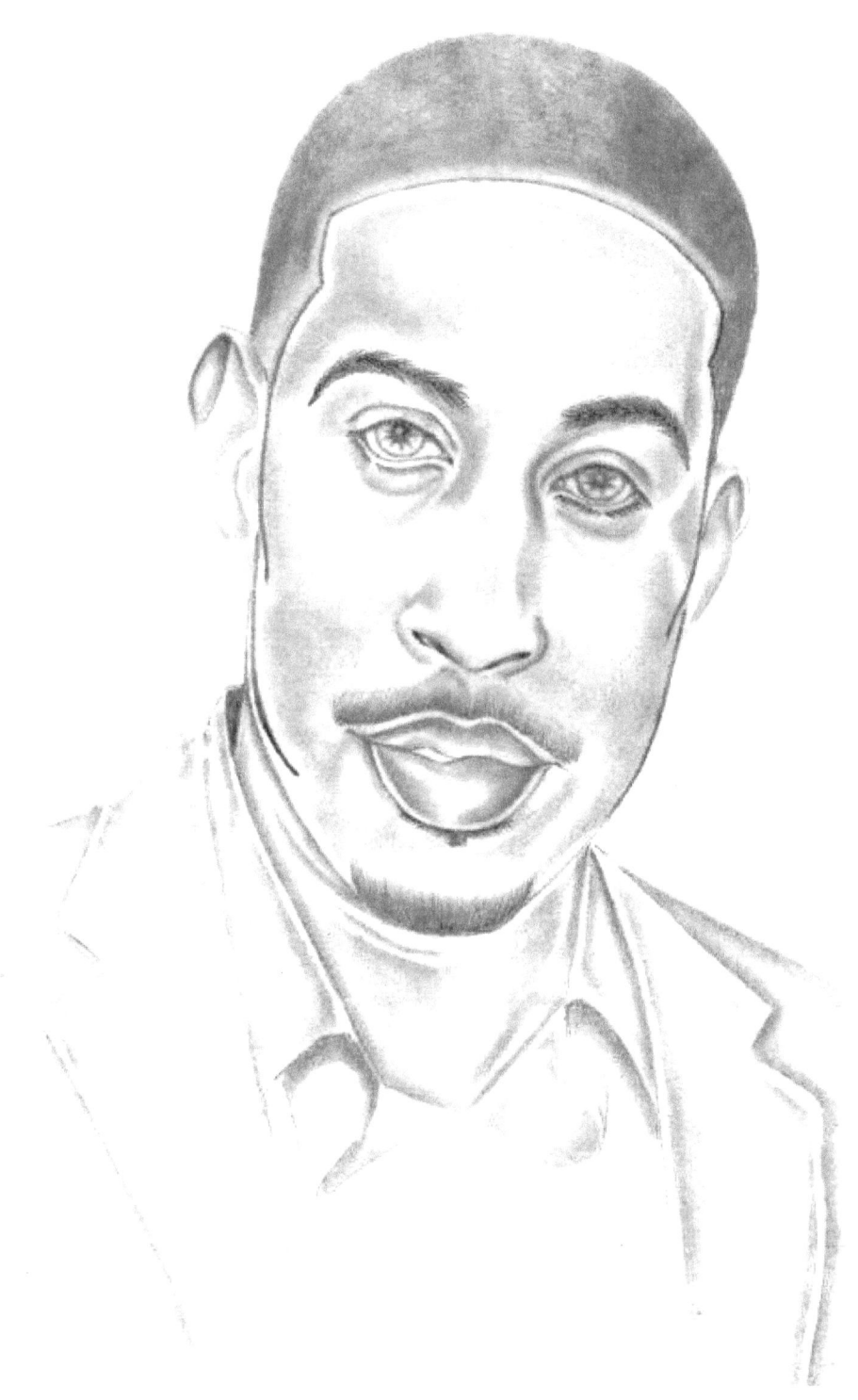

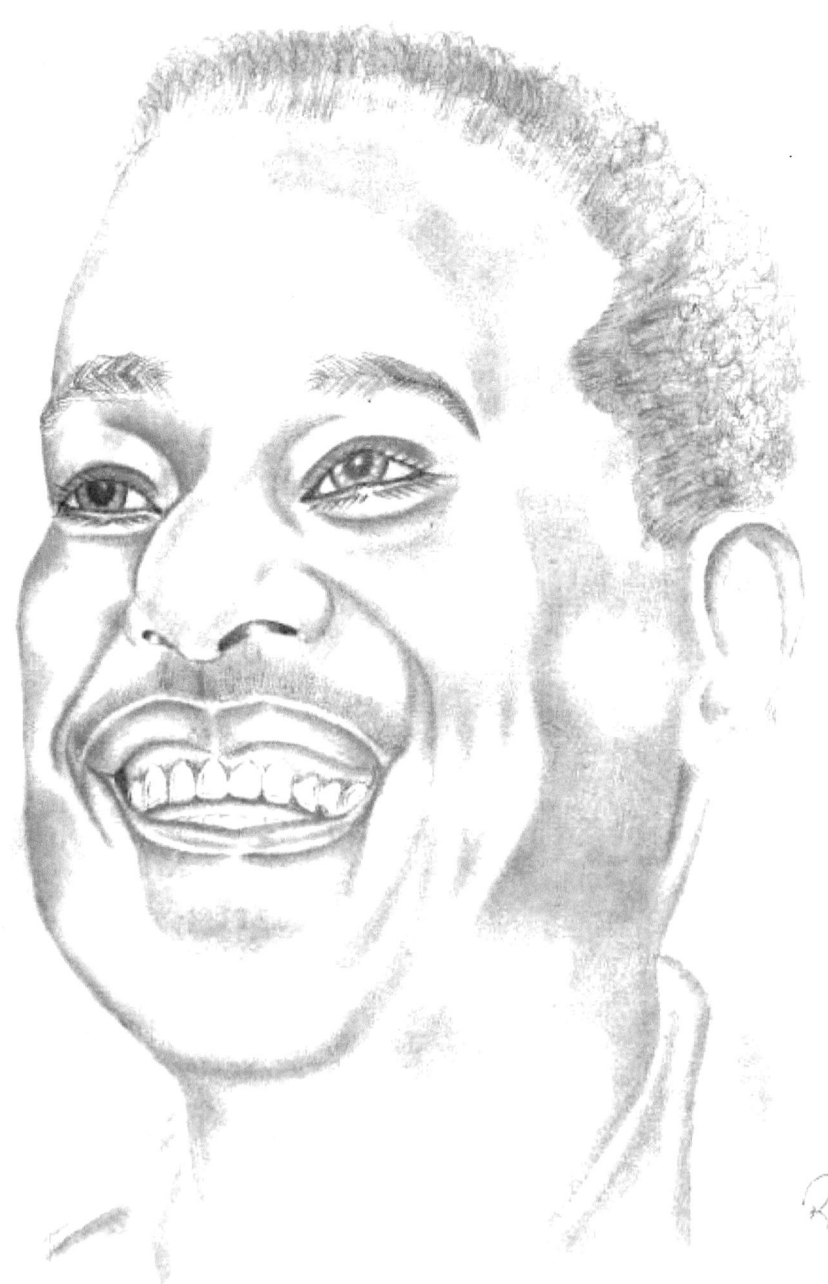

Reginald O.

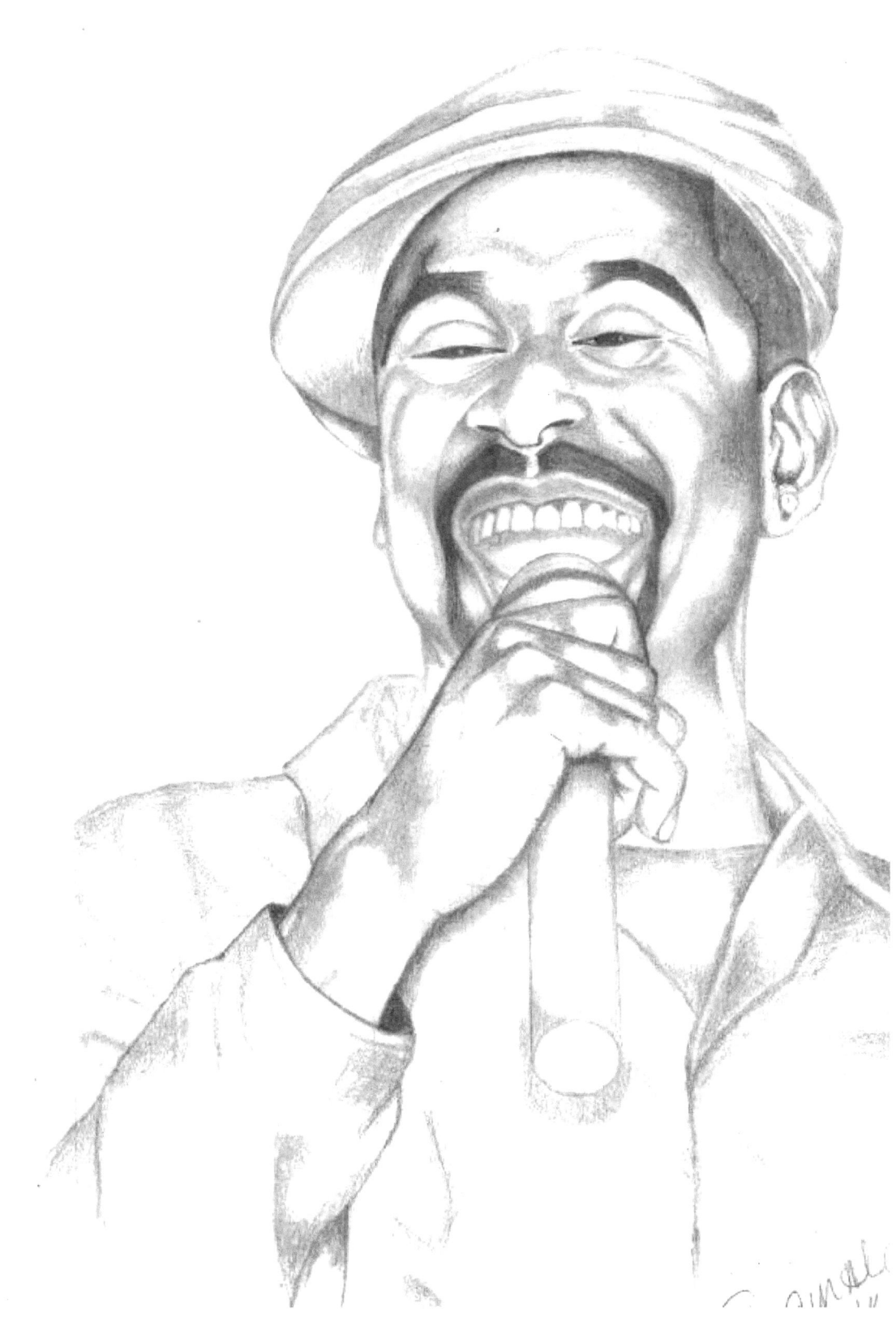

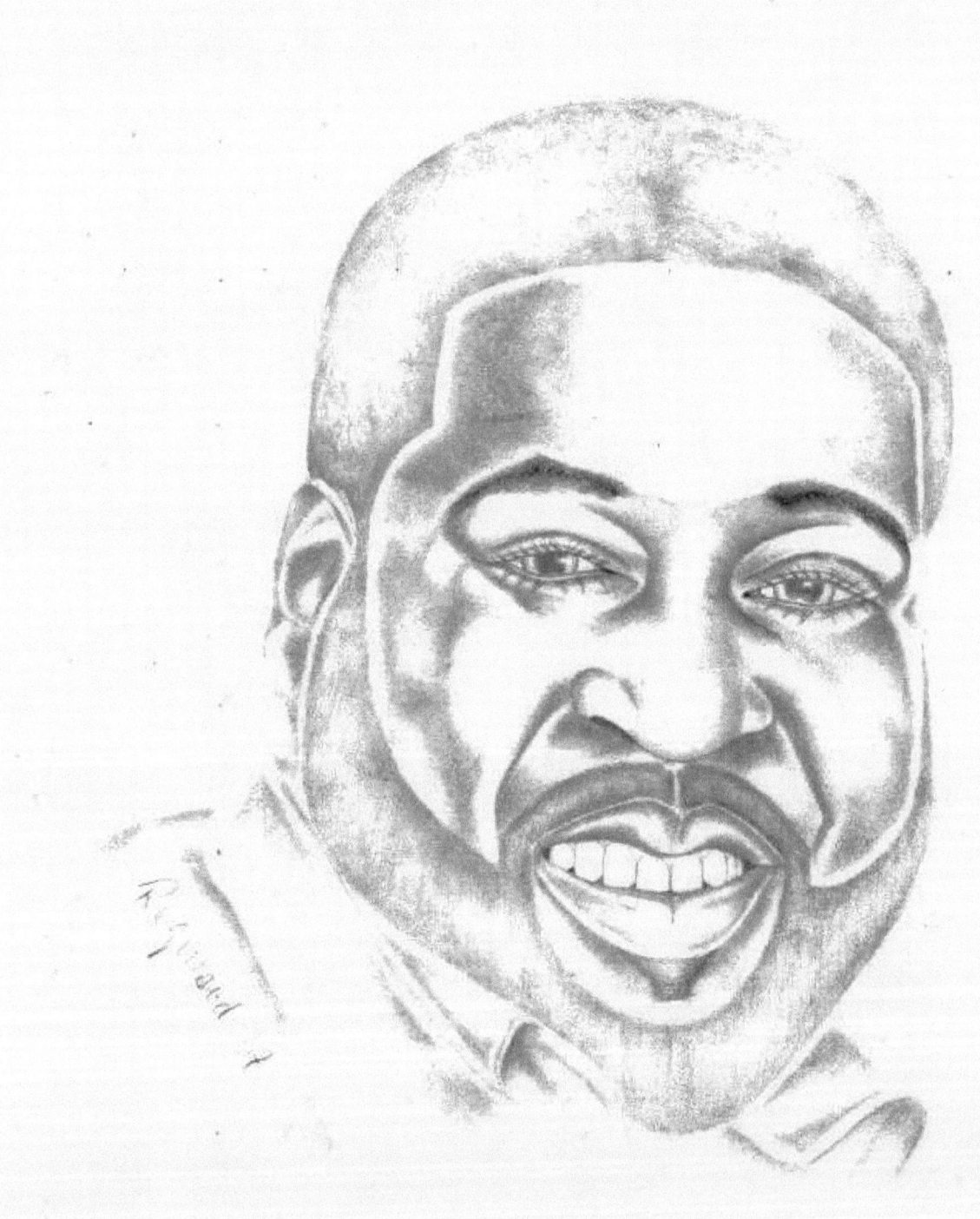

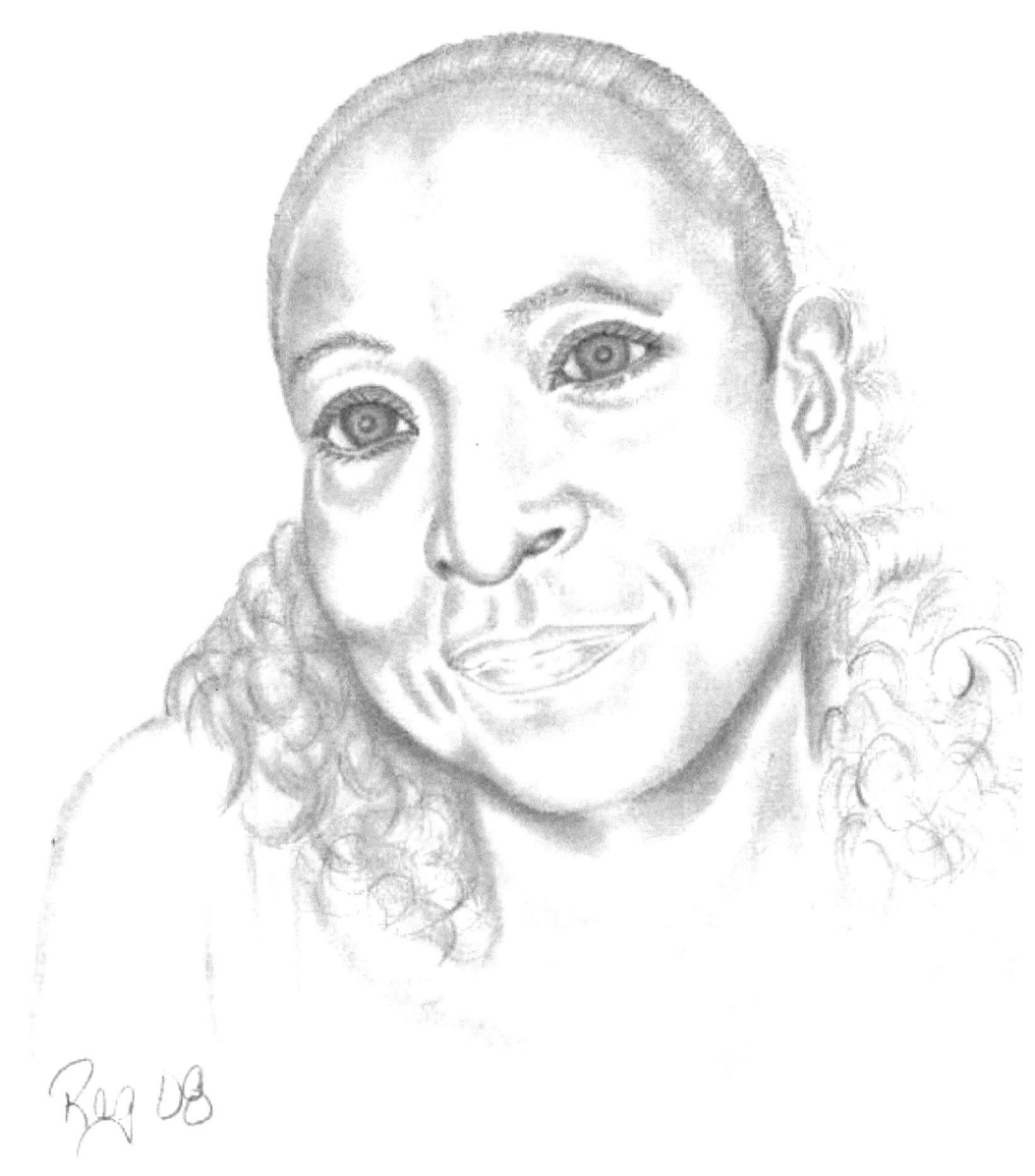

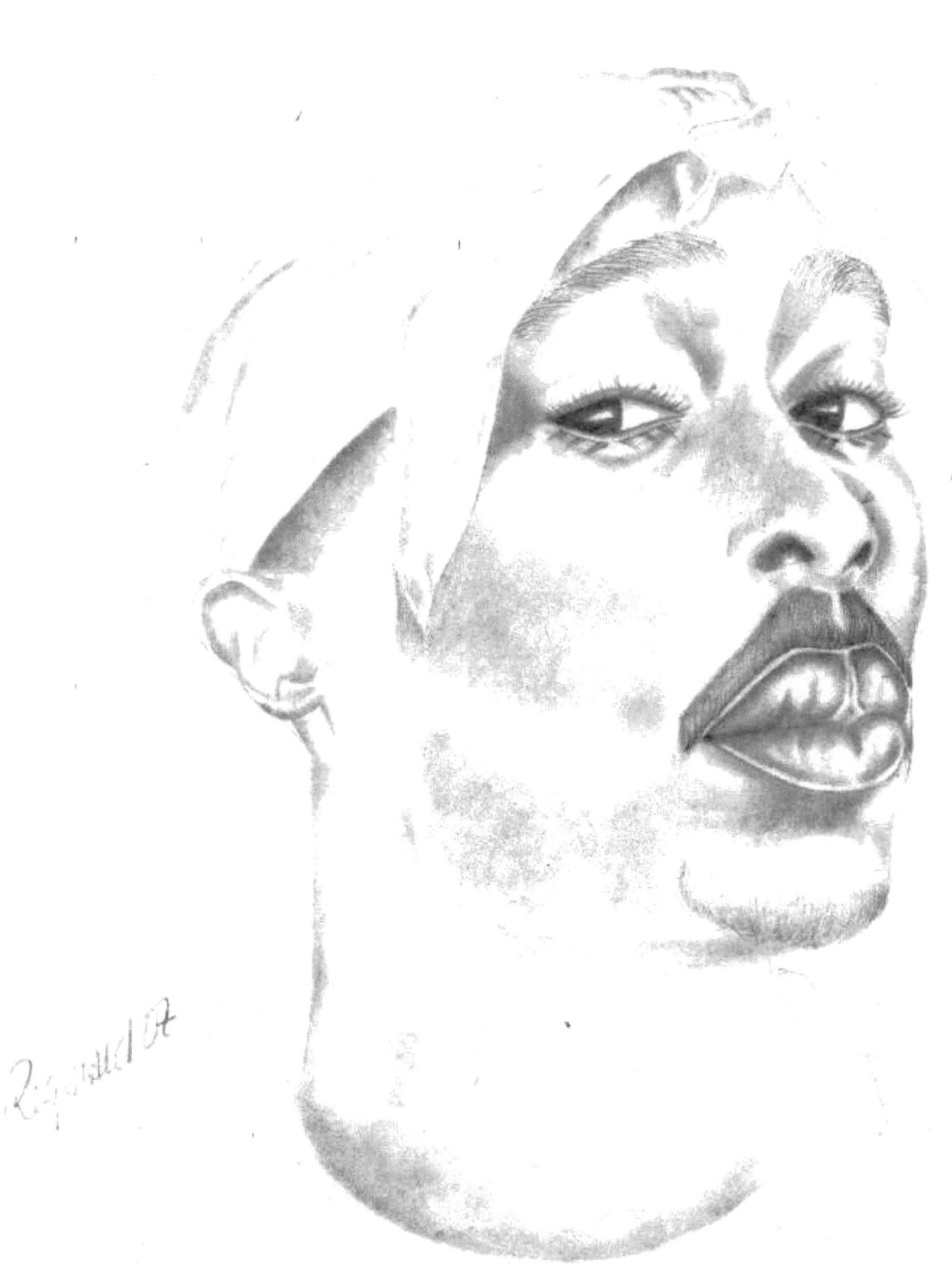

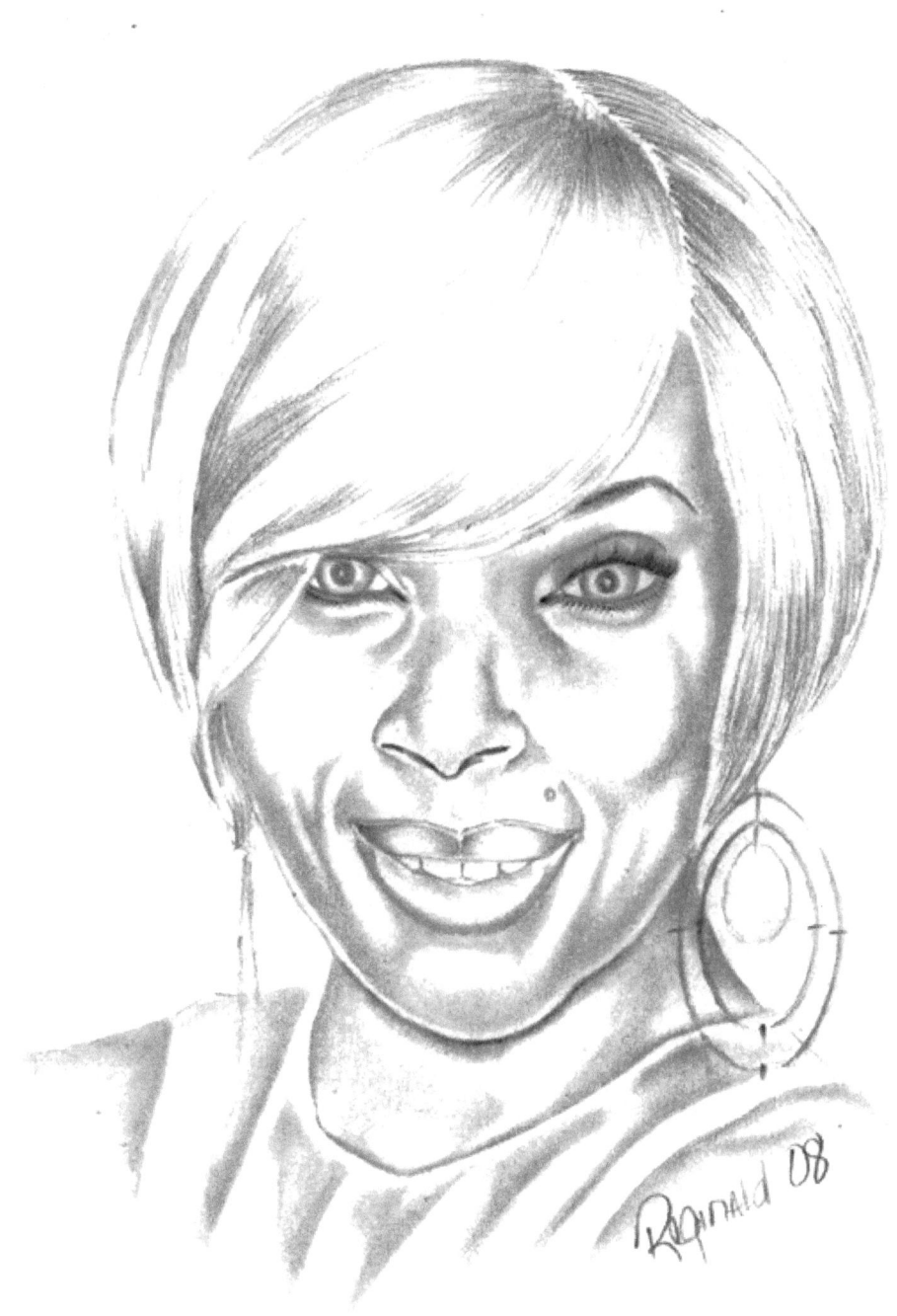

www.ingramcontent.com/pod-product-compliance
Lightning Source LLC
Chambersburg PA
CBHW040756200526

45159CB00026B/2666